Green Finance Tools: A Practical Guide to Sustainable Investment Instruments, Climate Risk Mitigation, and Blended Finance Strategies

I0040385

Copyright

Copyright © 2025 by Robert C. Brears

All rights reserved.

No part of this publication may be reproduced, stored in a retrieval system, or transmitted in any form or by any means—electronic, mechanical, photocopying, recording, or otherwise—without the prior written permission of the publisher, except in the case of brief quotations embodied in critical articles or reviews.

First edition published in 2025 by

Global Climate Solutions

ISBN 978-1-991369-35-2 (eBook)

ISBN 978-1-991369-36-9 (paperback)

This book is a work of nonfiction. While every effort has been made to ensure accuracy, the author and publisher disclaim any liability for errors or omissions. The content is intended for informational purposes only and does not constitute financial, legal, or investment advice.

The views expressed in this publication represent the perspectives of the author and are shared by the publisher.

Cover design and interior layout by Global Climate Solutions.

Table of Contents

Preface

The global shift toward sustainability is transforming the way capital is mobilized, managed, and measured. As climate change, biodiversity loss, and environmental degradation rise to the top of policy and business agendas, green finance has become central to the design and delivery of solutions. From institutional investors and development finance institutions to regulators and fintech innovators, stakeholders across sectors are increasingly seeking clarity on the tools available to finance the transition to a low-carbon, climate-resilient economy.

This book was written to provide that clarity.

Green Finance Tools offers a practical, accessible guide to the wide range of instruments now used to fund environmentally sustainable activities. It is structured around the tools themselves—green bonds, sustainability-linked loans, carbon markets, guarantees, public finance mechanisms, digital innovations, and more—each presented with a focus on how they work, where they apply, and what challenges and opportunities they present. The aim is to support professionals who need structured insights into the mechanics of green finance without relying on case studies or region-specific narratives.

The audience for this book includes practitioners in climate and sustainability policy, ESG and impact investing, development banking, financial regulation, and project finance. It may also serve as a reference for academics, students, and early-career professionals seeking to understand how financial instruments interact with climate goals, environmental safeguards, and emerging disclosure standards.

The content is grounded in neutral, current language and designed for use across both developed and emerging markets. It does not assume prior expertise in finance or environmental policy, though it is written with the expectation that the reader is engaged in sustainability-related work.

As the landscape of green finance continues to evolve, there will be a need for continuous learning, collaboration, and refinement of the tools we use. It is my hope that this book contributes to that process by serving as a clear, organized reference point for those working to align finance with the needs of people, planet, and future generations.

— Robert C. Brears

Introduction

Green finance refers to the allocation of financial resources toward projects, assets, and activities that contribute to environmental sustainability. It encompasses a broad range of instruments and mechanisms designed to support the transition to a low-carbon, climate-resilient, and resource-efficient economy. These include, but are not limited to, green bonds, sustainability-linked loans, carbon markets, and green investment funds. Green finance operates at the intersection of the financial system and environmental goals, facilitating investments that align with international climate commitments, such as the Paris Agreement, and sustainability frameworks like the United Nations Sustainable Development Goals (SDGs). The scope of green finance extends beyond mitigation efforts to include adaptation, conservation of biodiversity, and sustainable use of natural resources. As both public and private financial actors increasingly recognize environmental risks and opportunities, green finance plays a vital role in redirecting capital flows toward sustainable development pathways.

Objective of the Book

The purpose of this book is to provide a comprehensive overview of the key tools that drive green finance. Rather than focusing on general discussions or case studies, the book is structured to offer clear, concise insights into specific instruments and mechanisms currently shaping the green finance landscape. Each chapter is dedicated to one tool or category of tools, exploring its structure, function, challenges, and potential. By providing this focused and tool-based approach, the book aims to serve as a practical resource for professionals, researchers, and policymakers seeking to better understand and engage with green financial mechanisms.

Overview of Chapters

The book begins with a detailed look at green bonds, one of the most established tools in the green finance space. It then explores sustainability-linked instruments, such as bonds and loans tied to environmental performance targets. Following this, the book examines green loans and credit lines, particularly in relation to SMEs and household financing. The fourth chapter focuses on green investment funds, including institutional and retail structures. The fifth chapter reviews carbon markets and offsetting mechanisms. Chapter six discusses guarantees, insurance, and risk-sharing instruments that mitigate financial uncertainty in green investments. Taxonomies, standards, and disclosure tools are analyzed in chapter seven. Chapter eight shifts attention to public finance and blended finance instruments, while the final chapter highlights the growing role of fintech and digital innovation in green finance, including tools designed for retail investors. Collectively, the chapters offer a wide-ranging overview of how green finance tools are mobilized and scaled globally.

Importance of Tool-Based Approach

A tool-based approach allows for a practical and structured understanding of green finance, offering clarity in a rapidly evolving field. By isolating individual financial mechanisms and exploring their specific characteristics, this format enables readers to distinguish between types of instruments, their roles, and their limitations. This approach also highlights how these tools interact and complement each other within the broader financial system. In doing so, it supports informed decision-making, policy development, and implementation by financial institutions, regulators, and stakeholders seeking to align capital with sustainability objectives in a coherent and transparent manner.

Chapter 1: Green Bonds

Green bonds have emerged as one of the most prominent and widely used instruments in green finance. These fixed-income securities are specifically designed to raise capital for projects with environmental benefits, including renewable energy, energy efficiency, sustainable water management, and climate adaptation. The growth of the green bond market reflects increasing investor demand for sustainable investment options and the broader shift within financial systems toward supporting low-carbon development. This chapter provides a detailed overview of the structure, issuance process, market dynamics, and challenges associated with green bonds, offering a foundation for understanding their role within the broader suite of green finance tools.

What Are Green Bonds?

Green bonds are debt instruments issued to raise capital specifically for projects that deliver environmental benefits. Similar to conventional bonds in terms of structure and repayment, green bonds are distinguished by the commitment that the proceeds will be used exclusively for environmentally sustainable activities. These activities may include renewable energy generation, energy efficiency upgrades, sustainable transportation systems, waste management, water resource conservation, and climate change adaptation measures. The underlying financial characteristics—such as interest rates, maturity periods, and repayment obligations—are typically aligned with those of traditional fixed-income securities.

The concept of green bonds emerged in the late 2000s, with early issuances by multilateral development banks, including the European Investment Bank (EIB) and the World Bank. Since then, the market has grown significantly, encompassing sovereign, sub-sovereign, corporate, and financial institution issuers. Green bonds have become a central pillar in the broader green finance ecosystem, offering both public and private sector entities a mechanism to signal environmental intent while accessing diverse pools of capital.

The issuance of a green bond generally requires a framework that outlines how the funds will be allocated, how the projects will be evaluated and selected, and how reporting on the environmental impact will be conducted. These frameworks are often aligned with established voluntary standards, such as the Green Bond Principles (GBP) developed by the International Capital Market Association (ICMA). External reviews, including second-party opinions and certifications, may be sought to enhance credibility and transparency, though such reviews are not mandatory.

From the investor's perspective, green bonds offer an opportunity to support environmental outcomes without deviating from traditional risk-return expectations. For issuers, they can attract environmentally conscious investors, enhance reputation, and potentially access a broader or more loyal investor base. However, questions around the definition of "green" and the potential for misuse of proceeds—commonly referred to as "greenwashing"— have underscored the importance of clear disclosure, credible governance, and transparent reporting.

Overall, green bonds serve as a foundational tool in the mobilization of capital for sustainable development. They align financial flows with climate and environmental objectives, supporting national and international goals such as the Paris Agreement and the SDGs. As regulatory frameworks and market expectations continue to evolve, green bonds are likely to remain a central feature of the sustainable finance landscape.

Structure and Use-of-Proceeds Model

The defining feature of green bonds lies in their use-of-proceeds model, which mandates that capital raised through issuance is allocated exclusively to projects with demonstrable environmental benefits. This model forms the core distinction between green bonds and conventional bonds. While the financial characteristics—such as coupon rate, maturity, and repayment structure—may be similar to those of traditional fixed-income instruments, the additional layer of purpose-driven financing introduces both opportunities and responsibilities for issuers and investors.

Under the use-of-proceeds model, issuers commit to earmarking bond proceeds for eligible green projects. These may include initiatives in renewable energy, energy efficiency, pollution prevention, clean transportation, sustainable water and wastewater management, climate change adaptation, and the preservation of biodiversity. Some issuers expand their frameworks to include circular economy projects or green buildings that meet specific certification standards. The project eligibility criteria are typically detailed in a green bond framework, which outlines how the issuer defines "green" and the types of projects it intends to finance.

The GBP, developed by the IMCA, serve as a widely accepted voluntary framework for structuring green bonds. The GBP provide guidance through four core components: (1) use of proceeds, (2) project evaluation and selection, (3) management of proceeds, and (4) reporting. Issuers following these principles are expected to clearly communicate how proceeds will be allocated, provide transparency on project selection, maintain internal controls to track fund disbursement, and report on the environmental impacts of the financed activities.

In practice, the management of proceeds is usually carried out through a dedicated sub-account or internal tracking system. Funds may be temporarily invested in cash or liquid instruments until they are fully deployed. This process ensures that proceeds are not commingled with general funds, reinforcing investor confidence in the bond's environmental claims.

To further enhance credibility and market acceptance, many issuers obtain external reviews. These may include second-party opinions, third-party verifications, or certifications from independent bodies.

External reviewers typically assess whether the green bond framework aligns with accepted standards and whether the proposed use of proceeds and reporting mechanisms are robust. While such reviews are not mandatory, they have become common market practice, particularly among repeat issuers and those targeting institutional investors.

Post-issuance, issuers are expected to publish regular reports—often annually—detailing the allocation of proceeds and, where possible, the environmental performance or impact of the funded projects. Metrics might include reductions in greenhouse gas emissions, energy savings, or improvements in water quality, depending on the nature of the projects.

The use-of-proceeds model not only facilitates transparency and accountability but also plays a crucial role in shaping investor expectations. By ensuring that funds are directed toward clearly defined environmental outcomes, this model has helped establish green bonds as a credible and reliable instrument for sustainable investment. As regulatory standards and data requirements evolve, the structure underpinning green bonds continues to mature, supporting greater alignment between finance and sustainability goals.

Issuers and Markets

The green bond market has grown from a niche initiative into a mainstream component of global fixed-income markets. A diverse range of issuers now participate in the green bond space, including sovereign governments, subnational authorities, multilateral development banks, corporations, and financial institutions. This breadth reflects increasing awareness of environmental challenges and the role of capital markets in addressing sustainability goals.

Sovereign issuers have played a growing role in setting benchmarks for national climate policy and signaling long-term commitments to sustainable development. Governments issue green bonds to finance public sector infrastructure, energy, and environmental projects aligned with climate targets. Examples include renewable energy installations, low-carbon transport systems, and climate adaptation programs. Sovereign green bonds also serve as a model for subnational and private sector issuers, encouraging broader market participation.

Municipal and sub-sovereign entities—such as cities, states, and provinces—are also active in issuing green bonds. These bonds often support urban sustainability initiatives, such as energy-efficient public buildings, stormwater infrastructure, or sustainable mobility projects. Local issuance reflects the decentralization of environmental responsibilities and highlights the role of cities in implementing climate strategies.

Multilateral development banks (MDBs) were among the first institutions to issue green bonds, laying the groundwork for the current market. Institutions like the World Bank and the European Investment Bank have maintained high levels of credibility and transparency in their green bond programs. MDBs continue to play an important catalytic role by supporting capacity-building, facilitating investor confidence, and standardizing good practices across the market.

Corporate issuers have increasingly turned to green bonds to finance transitions in their business models, particularly in energy, manufacturing, real estate, and utilities. Green bonds allow corporations to align their capital expenditure with sustainability objectives while accessing environmentally focused investors. Issuers are expected to disclose how the financed projects fit within their overall sustainability strategies, reinforcing market discipline.

Financial institutions, including commercial banks, often issue green bonds to on-lend to eligible green projects or clients. These institutions act as intermediaries in scaling capital flows to sustainable sectors, such as renewable energy, green construction, or electric mobility. Their participation deepens the market and contributes to diversification of green bond portfolios.

The global green bond market has developed across multiple currencies and geographies, supported by exchanges offering green bond listings, transparency platforms, and indexes. Market growth has been further supported by regulatory encouragement, voluntary guidelines, and investor demand for ESG-aligned assets. As the market matures, attention is increasingly focused on harmonization of standards, consistency in reporting, and the integration of green bonds within broader sustainable finance taxonomies.

Certification, Verification, and Standards

Certification, verification, and adherence to standards are critical elements in ensuring the integrity and credibility of green bonds. These mechanisms help build market confidence by providing assurance that the proceeds from green bond issuances are directed toward projects with clear and measurable environmental benefits. While green bond standards are largely voluntary, they play an essential role in establishing common expectations, improving transparency, and mitigating the risk of mislabeling or "greenwashing."

The GBP, developed by the IMCA, are the most widely recognized voluntary guidelines for green bond issuance. The GBP set out four core components: (1) use of proceeds, (2) process for project evaluation and selection, (3) management of proceeds, and (4) reporting. Issuers who align with the GBP are expected to publish a green bond framework outlining how they address these components. Although not legally binding, the principles are widely adopted by issuers and serve as a benchmark for investor due diligence.

To enhance transparency and provide third-party assessment, many issuers seek external reviews. These reviews fall into several categories, including second-party opinions, verification, certification, and green bond ratings. A second-party opinion is typically issued by a sustainability consultancy or research organization. It assesses the alignment of the issuer's framework with the GBP or other standards and evaluates the environmental robustness of the proposed projects. These opinions are published prior to issuance and often made publicly available to support investor evaluation.

Verification involves confirming specific claims made by the issuer, such as the use of proceeds or the environmental impact of the financed projects. This may be done at issuance and during post-issuance reporting. Some issuers also seek certification under recognized standards, such as the Climate Bonds Standard (CBS), developed by the Climate Bonds Initiative. The CBS provides a science-based taxonomy of eligible projects and requires third-party verification for certification. Certified bonds must adhere to pre- and post-issuance requirements, including annual reporting.

Green bond ratings, offered by some credit rating agencies, assess the environmental and sustainability credentials of a bond or its framework. These ratings are distinct from traditional credit ratings and are not yet universally adopted but may serve as an additional signal of credibility.

The availability and quality of external reviews vary by region, issuer size, and market maturity. While these tools add to the cost and complexity of issuance, they are increasingly viewed as essential for maintaining market discipline and protecting the long-term viability of the green bond market. Investors often rely on such reviews to compare bonds, assess risks, and make informed investment decisions.

As green finance continues to evolve, efforts to standardize and harmonize certification and verification processes are gaining momentum. Initiatives by regulators, standard-setting bodies, and multilateral institutions are supporting the development of more consistent global frameworks. These developments aim to reduce fragmentation, improve comparability, and support the credibility and growth of the green bond market.

Benefits and Challenges

Green bonds offer a range of benefits to both issuers and investors, while also presenting certain challenges that affect their broader adoption and long-term effectiveness. As a financing tool, green bonds contribute to aligning capital markets with environmental objectives, yet their performance depends on regulatory clarity, market maturity, and stakeholder expectations.

From the issuer's perspective, green bonds can attract a diversified investor base, particularly those with environmental, social, and governance (ESG) mandates. The issuance of green bonds may enhance an organization's reputation, demonstrating a commitment to sustainability and corporate responsibility. In some cases, green bonds can help issuers achieve more favorable pricing or increase demand, although evidence of a consistent "greenium" (green premium) remains mixed. Issuers also benefit from the internal process of identifying eligible projects, which may contribute to improved sustainability governance and long-term planning.

For investors, green bonds provide an opportunity to support environmentally beneficial activities without deviating from traditional fixed-income strategies. Investors gain access to sustainable assets with credit profiles similar to conventional bonds, allowing for portfolio diversification with environmental impact. Transparent reporting requirements and external reviews further support investor confidence and risk assessment.

Despite these advantages, several challenges remain. One key issue is the lack of a universally accepted definition of what qualifies as a "green" project. This ambiguity may lead to inconsistencies in how green bonds are structured and reported, creating difficulties for investors seeking comparability across issuers and markets. The risk of greenwashing—where the environmental credentials of a bond are overstated—can undermine trust in the market, particularly in the absence of strong oversight or independent verification.

Another challenge is the cost and complexity of issuance. Complying with green bond principles, obtaining external reviews, and conducting post-issuance reporting require additional time and resources. For smaller issuers or those in developing markets, these barriers may be significant and discourage participation.

There is also an ongoing debate about the additionality of green bonds—whether they finance projects that would not have occurred otherwise. Critics argue that labeling existing investments as "green" may not meaningfully accelerate climate action unless accompanied by systemic change in capital allocation.

In summary, while green bonds are a useful and increasingly popular tool for sustainable finance, addressing these challenges will be essential to ensuring their continued growth, credibility, and effectiveness in supporting environmental goals.

Evolution into Thematic Bonds

The green bond market has evolved over time to include a broader range of sustainability-focused debt instruments, commonly referred to as thematic bonds. These instruments follow a similar structure to green bonds but target a wider set of environmental and social objectives. The expansion of thematic bonds reflects growing investor interest in addressing interconnected sustainability challenges through capital markets.

Thematic bonds now include social bonds, which finance projects with positive social outcomes, such as affordable housing, access to education, or healthcare. Additionally, sustainability bonds combine both environmental and social goals, allowing issuers to support a range of eligible activities under a single framework. These instruments broaden the appeal of sustainable finance to a wider group of issuers and investors.

More recently, blue bonds have emerged as a subset of green bonds, focusing on the sustainable use of ocean and marine resources. These instruments are gaining attention in coastal and island nations that rely heavily on marine ecosystems for economic development and climate resilience.

The development of thematic bonds has been supported by voluntary guidelines, such as the Social Bond Principles and Sustainability Bond Guidelines issued by ICMA. These frameworks mirror the structure of the Green Bond Principles, emphasizing transparency, use of proceeds, and impact reporting.

As thematic bonds gain momentum, they contribute to the diversification of the sustainable debt market. This evolution allows for more nuanced financial instruments that align with specific development goals, while retaining the credibility and transparency mechanisms established in the green bond market.

Chapter 2: Sustainability-Linked Instruments

Sustainability-linked instruments represent a relatively recent innovation in the sustainable finance market. Unlike green bonds or loans, which require proceeds to be allocated to specific environmental projects, sustainability-linked instruments are tied to an issuer's overall sustainability performance. These tools link financial terms—such as interest rates or repayment conditions—to the achievement of predefined environmental, social, or governance (ESG) targets. This chapter explores the key features, structures, and applications of sustainability-linked bonds and loans, highlighting their flexibility and potential to support corporate and institutional transitions toward long-term sustainability goals.

Overview of Sustainability-Linked Instruments

Sustainability-linked instruments are financial products that connect an issuer's financing costs or conditions to the achievement of predefined sustainability performance objectives. Unlike green bonds or loans, which require the proceeds to be directed toward specific eligible projects, sustainability-linked instruments are general-purpose financing tools. Their distinguishing feature lies in the integration of sustainability performance targets (SPTs) that reflect the issuer's broader environmental, social, or governance (ESG) goals.

The most common types of sustainability-linked instruments include sustainability-linked bonds (SLBs) and sustainability-linked loans (SLLs). These instruments incorporate financial or structural adjustments—such as interest rate step-ups or step-downs—based on whether the issuer meets or fails to meet agreed-upon key performance indicators (KPIs) within a specified timeline. This approach incentivizes improved ESG performance by linking it directly to financial terms, while also providing issuers with flexibility in how they use the proceeds.

The market for sustainability-linked instruments has expanded rapidly since the release of the Sustainability-Linked Bond Principles (SLBP) and Sustainability-Linked Loan Principles (SLLP), developed by the IMCA and the Loan Market Association (LMA), respectively. These voluntary guidelines outline five core components: (1) selection of KPIs, (2) calibration of SPTs, (3) bond or loan characteristics, (4) reporting, and (5) verification. Adherence to these principles is seen as good practice and supports transparency and market integrity.

Sustainability-linked instruments are particularly relevant for issuers in transition sectors—such as energy, manufacturing, or transportation—where aligning business models with long-term sustainability goals requires phased, company-wide changes. These instruments allow issuers to demonstrate commitment to ESG objectives while maintaining operational and capital allocation flexibility.

Investor interest in sustainability-linked instruments continues to grow, driven by the desire to engage with issuers on long-term performance and impact. However, the effectiveness of these tools depends on the credibility of KPIs, the ambition of the performance targets, and the robustness of monitoring and reporting mechanisms.

As the sustainable finance market evolves, sustainability-linked instruments offer a complementary approach to project-based tools like green bonds. By embedding ESG outcomes into the core terms of financing, they support greater alignment between financial performance and sustainability objectives across a wider range of issuers and sectors.

KPIs and SPTs

The effectiveness of sustainability-linked instruments relies heavily on the selection and calibration of KPIs and SPTs. These components determine how an issuer's environmental, social, or governance (ESG) performance is measured and what level of improvement is expected over time. As such, KPIs and SPTs form the foundation of the financial and reputational integrity of sustainability-linked bonds and loans.

Key Performance Indicators are quantifiable metrics that track progress in specific ESG areas. Examples include greenhouse gas (GHG) emissions intensity, renewable energy usage, water consumption, waste reduction, workplace safety, or gender diversity in leadership roles. The KPIs selected must be material to the issuer's core operations, measurable using reliable data, and subject to consistent reporting over time. They should also align with recognized sustainability frameworks, such as the Global Reporting Initiative (GRI), Science Based Targets initiative (SBTi), or industry-specific standards.

Sustainability Performance Targets are time-bound goals that issuers commit to achieving in relation to their selected KPIs. These targets should be ambitious yet realistic, representing a meaningful improvement beyond business-as-usual practices. The credibility of an SPT depends on its alignment with external benchmarks, such as national climate commitments or sectoral pathways for decarbonization. SPTs should also reflect internal corporate strategy, ensuring integration into decision-making and operational planning.

The calibration of KPIs and SPTs is a critical step in structuring sustainability-linked instruments. It requires transparent justification of the targets' relevance, baseline year, and trajectory. Market participants, particularly investors, place significant emphasis on this aspect, as it determines whether the instrument drives real change or simply rewards existing commitments. Weak or insufficiently ambitious targets may lead to reputational risk for issuers and reduce the financial tool's credibility in the market.

In practice, issuers are encouraged to seek external reviews or second-party opinions to validate the materiality of KPIs and the ambition of SPTs. These assessments provide independent assurance to investors and other stakeholders that the instrument has been structured in line with established best practices.

Performance against SPTs is monitored throughout the life of the instrument. If the issuer fails to meet the targets, financial consequences—such as an increase in coupon or interest rate—are triggered. In some cases, outperformance may be rewarded through step-down mechanisms. Transparent reporting and verification of outcomes are essential for maintaining trust in these arrangements.

By linking financial terms to clear sustainability outcomes, KPIs and SPTs make sustainability-linked instruments a powerful mechanism for aligning financing with long-term ESG progress.

Market Adoption and Trends

Since their introduction, sustainability-linked instruments have gained notable traction across global financial markets. Both SLBs and SLLs are being increasingly adopted by a diverse set of issuers, including corporations, financial institutions, and public sector entities. Their growing popularity reflects the market's demand for flexible financing structures that align with long-term ESG goals.

The initial uptake of sustainability-linked loans was driven by large corporates seeking to embed ESG considerations into their corporate financing arrangements. These instruments were often tied to credit facilities or revolving lines of credit and used performance-based pricing adjustments to incentivize measurable improvements. Over time, sustainability-linked loans have become more standardized, with guidance from the LMA contributing to clearer expectations on target-setting, reporting, and verification.

Sustainability-linked bonds have followed a similar trajectory, though they are relatively newer in the market. Since the publication of the SLBP by the IMCA, there has been an increase in issuance volumes. Corporate issuers across various sectors—such as utilities, industrials, consumer goods, and real estate—are using SLBs to communicate sustainability commitments while maintaining flexibility in capital allocation. Some sovereigns and sub-sovereign entities have also begun exploring SLBs as a complement to their green bond programs.

One of the key trends shaping the market is the growing expectation around ambitious and credible sustainability performance targets. Investors and ESG analysts are increasingly scrutinizing the strength of targets and the rationale behind them. As a result, there is a shift toward the use of science-based or sector-specific benchmarks to ensure targets reflect genuine progress and avoid reputational concerns related to greenwashing.

Another trend is the integration of sustainability-linked features into broader financing strategies. Rather than treating these instruments as standalone products, issuers are embedding them into their sustainability-linked financing frameworks. These frameworks offer a consistent approach across multiple instruments and enhance internal alignment around ESG objectives.

Additionally, emerging markets are showing increased interest in adopting sustainability-linked instruments, supported by international financial institutions and blended finance platforms that provide technical assistance and risk mitigation. This trend has the potential to expand the reach of sustainability-linked finance beyond developed markets.

Looking ahead, continued innovation, regulatory engagement, and standardization efforts are likely to influence the evolution of this segment. As the market matures, sustainability-linked instruments are expected to play a significant role in driving accountability and progress across a broader set of ESG issues.

Risk of Greenwashing

As sustainability-linked instruments gain popularity, concerns about greenwashing—the practice of overstating or misrepresenting environmental or sustainability credentials—have become increasingly prominent. In the context of sustainability-linked bonds and loans, greenwashing risk arises when issuers commit to weak or unambitious SPTs, use vague or immaterial KPIs, or fail to transparently report progress over time. These issues can undermine the credibility of the instrument and erode trust among investors, regulators, and stakeholders.

One of the primary areas of concern is the selection of KPIs. If the chosen indicators do not reflect material sustainability challenges for the issuer's core operations, or if they represent improvements that would likely occur under normal business conditions, the financial linkage becomes symbolic rather than impactful. This raises questions about the instrument's additionality and the extent to which it drives genuine behavioral or operational change.

Another source of greenwashing risk involves unambitious or poorly calibrated SPTs. Targets that lack alignment with science-based benchmarks or sectoral decarbonization pathways may allow issuers to benefit from sustainability branding and favorable investor perception without undertaking meaningful transformation. This is especially problematic in transition sectors, where credibility depends on the robustness of the issuer's commitment to change.

The absence of standardized disclosure practices further complicates the issue. Without clear and consistent reporting frameworks, it can be difficult for investors to assess the relevance and effectiveness of selected KPIs, monitor progress, and compare issuers across the market. While voluntary principles such as those from ICMA and LMA encourage transparency and third-party verification, compliance is not mandatory, and practices vary widely.

To address these concerns, market participants are calling for greater accountability and oversight. This includes the use of second-party opinions to validate frameworks, increased scrutiny of SPT ambition, and more detailed post-issuance reporting. In some jurisdictions, regulators are beginning to explore guidance or requirements to enhance market discipline and protect investors from misleading sustainability claims.

Maintaining the credibility of sustainability-linked instruments will require continued focus on transparency, integrity, and ambition. As the market evolves, addressing the risk of greenwashing is essential to ensuring that these tools effectively contribute to sustainability outcomes and retain their value as credible components of the sustainable finance ecosystem.

Benefits and Flexibility

Sustainability-linked instruments offer several benefits that distinguish them from traditional green finance tools, particularly in terms of flexibility and alignment with broader sustainability strategies. By linking financial characteristics to predefined performance targets rather than specific project funding, these instruments provide issuers with a more adaptable approach to sustainable finance while maintaining accountability for ESG outcomes.

One of the key benefits is the general-purpose use of proceeds. Unlike green bonds or loans, which require proceeds to be allocated to eligible environmental projects, sustainability-linked instruments do not impose restrictions on how the capital is spent. This allows issuers to meet a variety of financing needs—such as working capital, refinancing, or growth initiatives—while still committing to measurable sustainability performance. The structure is particularly useful for companies undergoing broad ESG transitions or operating in sectors where project-level financing is not easily applicable.

Another important advantage is the alignment with long-term sustainability strategies. Sustainability-linked instruments encourage issuers to set performance targets that reflect company-wide ESG objectives, which may include carbon reduction, diversity improvements, or resource efficiency. This integration supports internal coherence between financing activities and broader corporate goals, enhancing transparency and stakeholder trust.

From an investor perspective, these instruments enable engagement with issuers on long-term impact without limiting investment to narrowly defined green activities. Investors can assess progress against KPIs and use that information to inform broader ESG integration or stewardship strategies. The inclusion of financial incentives, such as coupon step-ups or step-downs, provides a tangible mechanism for accountability and reinforces the link between ESG performance and financial outcomes.

Sustainability-linked instruments also contribute to market inclusivity. Entities that may lack sufficient green projects to justify a green bond or loan issuance can still access sustainable finance by committing to improve ESG performance at the organizational level. This opens the market to a wider range of participants, including those in transition sectors or smaller firms with limited green investment pipelines.

Despite their advantages, the effectiveness of sustainability-linked instruments depends on the credibility of selected KPIs and the ambition of performance targets. Transparent reporting and independent verification are essential for maintaining market confidence. When well-structured, these instruments offer a practical and scalable solution for integrating sustainability into mainstream financing.

Role in Transition Finance

Sustainability-linked instruments play a significant role in the broader context of transition finance, which aims to support the decarbonization and sustainability efforts of industries and companies that are not yet considered green but are working toward aligning with long-term climate and environmental goals. Unlike green finance, which typically focuses on low-carbon or environmentally beneficial activities already in place, transition finance emphasizes enabling change within existing high-emitting sectors by facilitating credible, science-based progress.

Sectors such as energy, steel, cement, aviation, shipping, and chemicals face complex challenges in reducing emissions due to their reliance on carbon-intensive processes. For many companies within these industries, allocating proceeds to traditional green projects may not be feasible or sufficient to reflect their full transition potential. In this context, SLBs and SLLs offer a flexible and impactful financing mechanism that aligns capital raising with meaningful emissions reductions and other ESG targets across an organization's operations.

By linking financial terms to specific SPTs, these instruments encourage companies to adopt transition pathways that are measurable, time-bound, and transparent. For example, a steel manufacturer may issue a sustainability-linked bond tied to reducing the carbon intensity of its production by a certain percentage over a fixed period. This approach provides financial motivation to meet ambitious targets while allowing the issuer to deploy proceeds according to broader operational needs.

Sustainability-linked instruments are also useful in signaling to stakeholders—including investors, regulators, and customers—that the issuer is committed to transformation. They provide a framework for accountability through ongoing performance monitoring and disclosure, helping build confidence that transition plans are not only aspirational but also operationalized through financial commitments.

In addition, these instruments contribute to the development of sector-specific transition finance frameworks, where credible transition criteria, benchmarks, and science-based targets are increasingly expected. As part of this trend, sustainability-linked instruments are being used to support alignment with net-zero roadmaps and national climate strategies, particularly in economies where energy and industrial transformation is central to achieving decarbonization objectives.

Overall, the role of sustainability-linked instruments in transition finance is to bridge the gap between current business models and future sustainability goals, providing a structured and flexible tool for mobilizing capital in support of long-term systemic change.

Chapter 3: Green Loans and Credit Lines

Green loans and credit lines are essential instruments within the sustainable finance landscape, enabling borrowers to access capital specifically for environmentally beneficial projects. Unlike sustainability-linked instruments, green loans are tied to the use of proceeds, requiring that funds be allocated to activities such as renewable energy, energy efficiency, and sustainable water or waste management. These instruments are applicable across various borrower types, including corporations, small and medium-sized enterprises (SMEs), public sector entities, and financial institutions. This chapter explores the structure, eligibility criteria, and deployment of green loans and green credit lines, as well as their role in supporting sustainable development across sectors and regions.

Introduction to Green Loans

Green loans are a form of debt financing specifically designed to fund projects that deliver clear and measurable environmental benefits. These instruments operate on the basis of the use-of-proceeds principle, meaning that borrowers must allocate the funds toward eligible green activities. The structure of green loans mirrors that of conventional loans, with standard terms related to interest rates, maturity, and repayment schedules. However, their defining feature is the environmental purpose for which the loan is issued.

Green loans are used to finance a wide range of projects, including renewable energy installations, energy efficiency upgrades, sustainable water and wastewater management, pollution prevention, clean transportation, green buildings, and biodiversity conservation. Depending on the borrower and the size of the project, green loans may take the form of bilateral agreements or syndicated facilities involving multiple lenders.

To ensure consistency and transparency in the market, the Green Loan Principles (GLP) were introduced by the LMA, in collaboration with other market participants. These principles provide voluntary guidelines for structuring, documenting, and reporting on green loans. The GLP are built around four key components: (1) use of proceeds, (2) project evaluation and selection, (3) management of proceeds, and (4) reporting. They align closely with the Green Bond Principles, providing a consistent framework across instruments.

One of the advantages of green loans is their adaptability to different borrower profiles. They are accessible not only to large corporations and public entities but also to SMEs, which often play a key role in local sustainability initiatives. In many cases, green loans are supported by public development banks or multilateral financial institutions, which offer technical assistance or concessional terms to improve affordability and reduce risk.

Green loans may also be structured as revolving credit facilities, particularly for clients with ongoing capital needs related to environmental performance. This format provides flexibility in disbursement and repayment, making it suitable for energy efficiency programs or infrastructure upgrades that occur in phases.

As demand for sustainable finance continues to grow, green loans are becoming an increasingly important mechanism for channeling capital toward environmental objectives. Their straightforward structure and alignment with established principles make them a practical tool for both borrowers and lenders seeking to contribute to sustainability goals through dedicated project finance.

Eligibility Criteria and Sectors

For a loan to qualify as a green loan, the underlying projects must meet clearly defined eligibility criteria that ensure alignment with environmental objectives. These criteria determine which activities can be financed under the green loan structure and help establish transparency, comparability, and credibility in the market. While definitions can vary across institutions and jurisdictions, many lenders and borrowers refer to the GLP and other recognized taxonomies to guide project selection.

According to the GLP, green projects must provide clear environmental benefits, which should be assessed, quantified where possible, and disclosed. The selection of eligible projects typically follows a documented process that includes internal review and, in some cases, external validation. This process enhances the integrity of the financing and supports investor and stakeholder confidence.

A wide range of sectors and activities may qualify under green loan frameworks. Common eligible sectors include:

- Renewable Energy: Projects involving wind, solar, hydro, geothermal, or other low-carbon energy sources.
- Energy Efficiency: Improvements to reduce energy consumption in buildings, industrial operations, or equipment.
- Pollution Prevention and Control: Initiatives aimed at reducing air, water, and soil pollution, including waste management and recycling.
- Sustainable Water and Wastewater Management: Projects that enhance water efficiency, treat wastewater, or promote sustainable water supply.
- Clean Transportation: Investments in electric vehicles, low-emission transport infrastructure, and modal shifts toward sustainable mobility.
- Green Buildings: New or refurbished buildings that meet recognized environmental standards (e.g., LEED, BREEAM, or national certifications).
- Climate Change Adaptation: Infrastructure or planning projects that enhance resilience to climate-related risks.
- Biodiversity and Conservation: Protection and restoration of natural ecosystems, reforestation, or habitat management.

In some instances, green loans may also support emerging categories, such as the circular economy, sustainable agriculture, or environmentally sustainable fisheries and aquaculture, depending on the institution's criteria and the borrower's sustainability strategy.

Eligibility criteria are typically defined in the borrower's green finance framework or in a dedicated loan agreement annex. These documents outline the specific categories applicable to the loan, the methodology for project evaluation, and the indicators used to assess environmental impact. Lenders may also require borrowers to report on the allocation and impact of proceeds, either through internal tracking systems or third-party assessments.

By establishing clear eligibility criteria and aligning them with recognized principles or taxonomies, green loans contribute to consistent market practices and support the broader goal of directing capital toward environmentally sustainable activities across key economic sectors.

Role of Commercial Banks and DFIs

Commercial banks and development finance institutions (DFIs) play a central role in the growth and accessibility of green loans across both developed and emerging markets. Their involvement ranges from direct lending to financial intermediation and capacity building, making them key enablers of capital flows toward environmentally sustainable activities.

Commercial banks serve as the primary channel for issuing green loans to a diverse base of borrowers, including corporations, SMEs, and public sector entities. These institutions develop internal green lending frameworks aligned with the GLP or other environmental standards to assess project eligibility and monitor the use of proceeds. Many commercial banks also establish dedicated sustainability units or committees to oversee the origination, structuring, and management of green loan portfolios.

Through their established relationships and credit evaluation capabilities, commercial banks are well-positioned to mainstream green lending into traditional financial services. They may offer green versions of conventional products, such as term loans, revolving credit facilities, and equipment financing, helping integrate environmental criteria into standard banking practices. In doing so, banks contribute to scaling up sustainable investment while supporting clients in transitioning to more sustainable operations.

Development finance institutions complement the role of commercial banks by providing long-term capital, risk mitigation tools, and technical assistance for green lending. DFIs often focus on markets or projects that face barriers to accessing finance due to perceived or actual risks. They play a critical role in developing green loan markets in low- and middle-income countries, where financial systems may be less mature and climate-aligned investments less developed.

DFIs support commercial banks through blended finance structures, where concessional capital is used alongside private investment to reduce risk and improve the financial viability of green projects. This approach helps mobilize private capital and encourages banks to lend to new sectors or clients that may not otherwise meet conventional credit criteria. DFIs also assist in capacity building, offering guidance on environmental screening, impact measurement, and alignment with international standards.

Both commercial banks and DFIs are increasingly integrating climate risk considerations into their lending practices. By incorporating environmental risk assessment tools, stress testing, and scenario analysis, these institutions enhance the resilience of their portfolios and contribute to systemic alignment with climate goals.

Together, commercial banks and DFIs form a collaborative ecosystem that advances the reach, quality, and integrity of green lending. Their combined efforts support the development of standardized practices, improve access to finance for environmentally beneficial projects, and facilitate the transition to a more sustainable financial system.

Green Lending for SMEs and Households

Green lending is increasingly being extended to SMEs and households, recognizing their collective potential to contribute to environmental sustainability and climate resilience. While green finance has traditionally focused on large-scale infrastructure or corporate projects, expanding access to smaller borrowers is critical to achieving broader sustainability objectives.

For SMEs, green loans can support a variety of activities such as upgrading to energy-efficient machinery, improving waste management systems, installing solar panels, or adopting cleaner production processes. SMEs often face structural barriers to accessing finance, including limited collateral, credit history constraints, and lack of awareness of green financing opportunities. To address these challenges, financial institutions are developing tailored green loan products with simplified application processes, technical support, and flexible repayment terms.

Development finance institutions and public programs often play a role in supporting green lending for SMEs through guarantees, concessional finance, or capacity-building initiatives. These mechanisms help reduce the perceived credit risk of SME lending while promoting the adoption of sustainable practices in local economies.

In the household sector, green loans are typically used for residential energy efficiency improvements, such as insulation upgrades, heat pump installations, or the purchase of efficient appliances. In some contexts, households may also access green loans for rooftop solar photovoltaic systems or water-saving technologies. These loans contribute to lower utility costs, improved living conditions, and reduced environmental footprints at the individual level.

Financial institutions are increasingly offering retail green loan products bundled with advisory services or linked to government incentive schemes. These offerings are often supported by public banks or national development programs, particularly in regions where sustainability is a policy priority. In some cases, green mortgages and home renovation loans are structured with preferential interest rates or repayment conditions based on the environmental performance of the property.

Digital platforms and fintech innovations are also playing a role in expanding green lending to underserved market segments. Online tools can support energy audits, loan applications, and monitoring of environmental impacts, helping bridge information gaps and improve accessibility.

By extending green lending to SMEs and households, financial institutions can support the democratization of green finance. This approach fosters more inclusive participation in the sustainability transition and enables the widespread adoption of environmentally responsible practices across all levels of the economy.

Blended Green Lending Models

Blended green lending models combine concessional finance from public or philanthropic sources with commercial capital to enhance the financial viability and scalability of environmentally sustainable projects. This approach is particularly relevant in contexts where market barriers—such as high upfront costs, perceived risk, or limited borrower capacity—prevent green investments from being financed under standard market conditions.

In blended structures, public institutions, including DFIs, climate funds, or government agencies, provide capital in the form of grants, guarantees, subordinated debt, or technical assistance. This capital is used to improve the risk-return profile of green lending opportunities for private sector lenders, encouraging them to participate in markets or borrower segments they may otherwise avoid. By absorbing higher risk or offering more favorable terms, concessional finance enables commercial lenders to extend credit to projects that align with environmental goals but fall outside conventional risk thresholds.

Blended green lending models are particularly effective in emerging markets, where access to affordable long-term finance is often constrained and the green finance ecosystem is still developing. For example, concessional funding may be used to establish a green credit line for local banks, which can then on-lend to small businesses or municipalities for eligible projects. Technical assistance components are often included to support loan origination, environmental assessment, and borrower capacity-building.

These models also play a role in supporting innovative or first-mover projects, such as pilot clean technology deployments or early-stage green infrastructure. By sharing risk, blended models help demonstrate financial viability, generate performance data, and attract follow-on investment from commercial sources once a project or technology is proven.

In addition to financial leverage, blended approaches promote market development by encouraging local financial institutions to build internal green finance capabilities. Participation in blended programs often involves alignment with international standards such as the Green Loan Principles or national green taxonomies, contributing to stronger governance and consistency in green lending practices.

Despite their benefits, blended green lending models require careful structuring to avoid market distortions, ensure transparency, and establish clear exit strategies for concessional partners. Proper design and implementation are essential to achieving both environmental impact and financial additionality.

Overall, blended green lending models are an important tool for accelerating the flow of capital to underfinanced sectors and regions, contributing to a more inclusive and effective green finance landscape.

Monitoring and Impact Reporting

Monitoring and impact reporting are essential components of green lending, providing transparency and accountability to ensure that loan proceeds are being used for their intended environmental purposes. These processes help lenders, borrowers, and stakeholders assess whether financed activities are achieving the anticipated outcomes, reinforcing the credibility and effectiveness of green loan instruments.

The GLP emphasize the importance of clear and ongoing communication regarding the use of proceeds and associated environmental impacts. Borrowers are expected to maintain records on how funds are allocated, including details about project implementation, disbursement status, and any changes to the planned activities. This internal tracking may be supported by designated sub-accounts, reporting systems, or project-level documentation.

Regular progress reports are typically required during the loan term. These may be submitted annually or at defined intervals, depending on the size and complexity of the project. Reports generally cover the allocation of proceeds, the status of financed activities, and environmental performance indicators. The level of detail may vary by institution, but common metrics include energy savings, renewable energy capacity installed, greenhouse gas emissions reduced or avoided, water conserved, or waste diverted from landfills.

Where feasible, borrowers are encouraged to use quantitative performance indicators and established methodologies to assess environmental benefits. This facilitates comparability across projects and enables aggregating results at the portfolio level. In cases where quantitative measurement is difficult, qualitative descriptions of outcomes may be provided, supported by narrative explanations or case-based evidence.

To enhance credibility, some lenders may require or recommend third-party verification or assurance of reported information. Independent auditors, environmental consultants, or verification agencies may be engaged to assess the accuracy and completeness of impact data, particularly for larger or high-profile loans. While not mandatory under the GLP, external reviews can increase confidence among investors and regulators and support reputational benefits for both lender and borrower.

Effective monitoring and impact reporting also contribute to learning and improvement, enabling institutions to refine project selection criteria, improve risk assessment, and strengthen internal sustainability processes. For public and blended finance programs, reporting is especially important to demonstrate alignment with policy goals and to support transparency in the use of public funds.

In sum, robust monitoring and impact reporting practices are fundamental to the success of green lending. They ensure that environmental objectives are met, build trust in the financial instrument, and support the broader development of a credible and data-driven green finance ecosystem.

Chapter 4: Green Investment Funds

Green investment funds serve as collective investment vehicles that allocate capital to projects, companies, or assets with positive environmental outcomes. These funds operate across a range of asset classes and investment strategies, including public equities, fixed income, and private equity. Managed by institutional investors, asset managers, or development finance institutions, green investment funds play an important role in mobilizing private capital at scale while promoting environmental sustainability. This chapter examines the structure, types, and strategies of green investment funds, as well as the role of investors, ESG integration, and evolving market practices.

Types of Green Funds

Green funds encompass a broad category of investment vehicles that direct capital toward environmentally sustainable activities. These funds vary in structure, scope, and strategy, catering to different investor profiles and sustainability objectives. While their core purpose is to support environmental goals, the specific approach taken can differ significantly depending on the fund's design and mandate.

One of the most common categories is green mutual funds, which pool money from retail and institutional investors to invest in publicly listed companies that meet specific environmental criteria. These funds typically apply ESG screening or integrate environmental factors into portfolio construction. Green mutual funds may track sustainability-focused indexes or be actively managed to select companies with strong environmental performance or climate-related business models.

Exchange-traded funds (ETFs) represent another widely used structure. Green ETFs offer diversified exposure to environmentally aligned companies or sectors, often with lower fees than actively managed funds. These instruments provide liquidity, transparency, and accessibility, making them popular among retail investors seeking to align their portfolios with environmental values. Some green ETFs focus on specific themes, such as clean energy, low-carbon technologies, or water conservation.

Private equity and venture capital green funds invest in early-stage or growth-stage companies developing clean technologies, renewable energy solutions, or nature-based innovations. These funds often take a long-term approach, providing not only capital but also strategic guidance to portfolio companies. Given their higher risk-return profile, these funds are typically targeted at institutional or accredited investors.

Green infrastructure funds focus on large-scale environmental projects, such as renewable energy generation, sustainable transport, or climate-resilient infrastructure. These funds may be structured as public-private partnerships and are commonly supported by development banks, pension funds, or sovereign wealth funds.

In addition, there are impact investment funds that explicitly seek measurable environmental outcomes alongside financial returns. These funds operate with dual mandates and often employ rigorous impact assessment frameworks to ensure that investments align with sustainability goals.

Lastly, blended finance green funds combine concessional capital from public sources with commercial investment to support projects in emerging or underserved markets. These funds aim to de-risk private investment and mobilize capital for activities that would otherwise be difficult to finance.

Together, these different types of green funds offer a diverse set of pathways for investors to contribute to environmental sustainability through pooled investment vehicles tailored to various risk preferences and strategic objectives.

Role of Institutional Investors

Institutional investors—including pension funds, insurance companies, sovereign wealth funds, and endowments—play a central role in advancing green investment through their substantial capital allocations and long-term investment horizons. As stewards of large pools of assets, these investors influence market trends and contribute to shaping the broader sustainable finance ecosystem.

Institutional investors are increasingly incorporating ESG considerations into their investment decision-making processes. Environmental factors—such as climate change risks, carbon emissions, and resource efficiency—have become a particular focus due to their potential impact on asset performance, valuation, and long-term portfolio resilience. This shift reflects a growing recognition that environmental risks can pose material financial risks and opportunities.

One of the key contributions of institutional investors is the allocation of capital to green funds, both as limited partners in private funds and as direct investors in public market products such as green ETFs and mutual funds. By channeling capital into funds that support renewable energy, sustainable infrastructure, and environmental innovation, institutional investors help scale up investment in green sectors. In doing so, they also signal to the market a demand for sustainable investment products, encouraging further fund development and standardization.

Institutional investors are also active in engagement and stewardship. Through proxy voting, dialogue with portfolio companies, and participation in collaborative investor initiatives, they can influence corporate behavior on environmental issues. Initiatives such as Climate Action 100+ and the Net-Zero Asset

Owner Alliance bring together institutional investors to collectively advocate for improved climate governance and disclosure.

In many jurisdictions, regulatory developments and fiduciary duty interpretations are reinforcing the importance of ESG integration for institutional investors. Some pension funds and sovereign wealth funds are required to report on the climate alignment of their portfolios or develop decarbonization strategies. These frameworks are creating momentum for further green investment and more transparent reporting practices.

Additionally, institutional investors contribute to market innovation by supporting the development of new green financial products, such as transition funds, nature-positive funds, or blended finance vehicles. Their participation can provide early-stage capital, validate fund structures, and enhance credibility in the eyes of other market participants.

Despite progress, challenges remain, including inconsistent ESG data, varying definitions of what constitutes "green," and the need for more scalable and investable green assets. Nonetheless, institutional investors are well-positioned to drive continued growth in green finance by leveraging their influence, scale, and long-term perspective to align capital flows with sustainability objectives.

Green ETFs and Mutual Funds

Green ETFs and green mutual funds are two of the most widely accessible investment vehicles for both retail and institutional investors seeking exposure to environmentally aligned assets. These pooled investment products allocate capital toward companies, sectors, or projects that meet predefined environmental criteria, often focusing on themes such as clean energy, energy efficiency, sustainable resource use, or low-carbon technologies.

Green mutual funds are typically actively managed and rely on portfolio managers to select investments based on a fund's environmental mandate. These funds may apply positive or negative ESG screening methods to include companies with strong environmental performance or exclude those involved in high-impact sectors such as fossil fuels or deforestation. The selection process often incorporates proprietary research, third-party ESG ratings, or thematic alignment with global frameworks such as the Paris Agreement or the UN Sustainable Development Goals.

In contrast, green ETFs are usually passively managed and track sustainability-focused indices. These indices may be constructed around specific environmental themes (e.g., renewable energy, water efficiency) or broader ESG integration criteria. Green ETFs provide investors with cost-effective, transparent, and liquid access to diversified portfolios of environmentally focused companies. Their standardized structure makes them particularly appealing for retail investors and asset allocators seeking exposure to sustainable investment strategies without incurring the higher fees typically associated with actively managed funds.

Both green ETFs and mutual funds play a key role in mainstreaming sustainable investment, allowing a wide range of investors to participate in environmental finance. They also facilitate capital market signaling, as inclusion in green indices or ESG-rated funds can enhance a company's visibility and attract sustainability-focused investment.

However, the growth of these funds has also raised concerns about consistency and comparability. The lack of harmonized definitions for what qualifies as "green" can lead to significant variation in fund composition, even among products with similar names or stated objectives. This has led to increased scrutiny from regulators and market participants, particularly regarding transparency, labeling practices, and alignment with underlying sustainability goals.

To address these challenges, efforts are underway to standardize fund classification systems, improve ESG disclosure requirements, and encourage greater transparency in fund methodologies.

Initiatives such as the EU's Sustainable Finance Disclosure Regulation (SFDR) aim to provide clearer information to investors about the environmental characteristics of financial products.

Overall, green ETFs and mutual funds represent important tools for mobilizing capital toward environmental objectives. Their accessibility, scalability, and growing investor demand position them as integral components of the evolving green finance landscape.

ESG Screening and Fiduciary Duty

ESG screening is a key tool used by green investment funds to evaluate and select portfolio holdings. ESG screening helps ensure that investments align with a fund's sustainability objectives by applying specific inclusion or exclusion criteria. In the context of green funds, environmental screening typically focuses on issues such as carbon emissions, renewable energy usage, pollution control, biodiversity impact, and resource efficiency.

There are two primary approaches to ESG screening: negative screening and positive screening. Negative screening excludes companies or sectors that are considered environmentally harmful, such as fossil fuel extraction, deforestation-linked industries, or those with poor environmental compliance records. Positive screening, on the other hand, involves selecting companies with strong environmental practices, innovative green technologies, or alignment with international sustainability frameworks.

An increasing number of asset managers and institutional investors are integrating ESG factors into their fiduciary duty, which refers to the obligation to act in the best interests of clients or beneficiaries. Historically, fiduciary duty was often interpreted narrowly, focusing primarily on financial returns. However, evolving market practices and regulatory guidance have expanded this interpretation to recognize that material ESG risks and opportunities can impact long-term financial performance.

As climate-related risks—such as physical damage, regulatory shifts, or market transitions—become more pronounced, investors are increasingly expected to assess and manage these risks as part of prudent investment practice. In many jurisdictions, regulatory bodies have clarified that ESG considerations are not only compatible with fiduciary duty but may be necessary to fulfill it. This development supports the broader integration of ESG screening into mainstream investment processes.

ESG screening also supports reputational and regulatory risk management. Funds that demonstrate a structured approach to sustainability may be better positioned to meet stakeholder expectations, comply with disclosure regulations, and avoid controversies linked to unsustainable practices. This is particularly relevant in the context of green investment funds, where transparency and consistency are critical to maintaining investor trust.

While ESG screening methods continue to evolve, the growing alignment between ESG integration and fiduciary responsibility reflects a broader shift in how investors approach risk, return, and long-term value. As standards and data quality improve, ESG screening is expected to become a core component of investment decision-making across the green finance sector.

Impact Investing Strategies

Impact investing refers to investment strategies that seek to generate both measurable environmental or social outcomes and financial returns. Within the context of green finance, impact investing focuses on directing capital toward projects, enterprises, or technologies that deliver tangible environmental benefits, such as reducing greenhouse gas emissions, improving water quality, restoring ecosystems, or enhancing climate resilience.

Impact investing differs from conventional ESG integration or sustainability-themed investing by emphasizing intentionality and measurability. The investor explicitly aims to achieve specific environmental outcomes and incorporates these objectives into the investment process from the outset. This approach often includes setting performance indicators, monitoring outcomes, and reporting on impact alongside financial results.

Impact strategies can be implemented across asset classes, including private equity, venture capital, fixed income, and real assets. They are commonly found in private market investments, where investors can work directly with companies or projects to influence operations and track outcomes. For example, an impact fund might invest in a company that develops off-grid solar solutions for rural communities, with metrics focused on energy access and emissions reductions.

To ensure accountability, many impact investors apply established impact measurement frameworks, such as the Impact Reporting and Investment Standards (IRIS+) or the Operating Principles for Impact Management. These tools help define what should be measured, how it should be measured, and how results should be communicated to stakeholders. This level of rigor is especially important in distinguishing impact investments from other forms of responsible or sustainable investing.

Green impact funds typically have a dual mandate: they aim to deliver financial returns in line with market expectations while achieving specific environmental targets. Some funds may accept slightly lower financial returns in exchange for higher environmental impact, especially in underserved or high-risk markets. However, many impact investors strive to demonstrate that positive impact and competitive financial performance are not mutually exclusive.

Institutional investors, development finance institutions, foundations, and family offices are among the most active participants in impact investing. Their involvement is helping to expand the market and build track records for green impact investments across regions and sectors.

As demand for accountability and measurable results increases, impact investing is gaining attention as a credible and structured approach to aligning capital with sustainability outcomes. Its emphasis on transparency, performance tracking, and intentional impact makes it a valuable tool within the broader green finance landscape.

Fund Lifecycle and Returns

The lifecycle of a green investment fund follows a structured process similar to that of traditional investment funds, encompassing stages from fundraising and capital deployment to portfolio management and exit. However, in green funds, each phase incorporates environmental objectives and performance considerations alongside financial goals.

The lifecycle typically begins with fundraising, during which fund managers define the investment thesis, target sectors, and expected environmental outcomes. This information is presented in offering documents and marketing materials to prospective investors, who may include institutional asset owners, development finance institutions, or high-net-worth individuals. Green funds may also establish environmental screening criteria, impact metrics, and alignment with frameworks such as the EU Taxonomy or SDGs as part of the fund's structure.

Once capital is committed, the fund moves into the investment phase, where managers source, evaluate, and select investments based on both financial and environmental criteria. Due diligence includes assessment of the project's or company's potential to deliver measurable environmental outcomes, manage risks, and comply with the fund's sustainability objectives. Investment decisions are supported by internal policies, sector expertise, and often third-party environmental assessments.

During the portfolio management phase, fund managers monitor financial performance and environmental impact in parallel. This involves regular reporting, engagement with investee companies, and adjustments as needed to maintain alignment with the fund's dual objectives. Transparent and consistent reporting is crucial, particularly for green funds that commit to delivering specific environmental outcomes.

Eventually, funds reach the exit phase, where they divest from portfolio assets through sales, public offerings, or other exit strategies. At this stage, fund managers aim to realize financial returns while assessing the longer-term sustainability of the impact generated. Exit decisions may also be influenced by changes in policy, market conditions, or investor preferences related to sustainability.

Green funds are typically benchmarked against traditional financial performance metrics, such as internal rate of return (IRR) or net asset value (NAV), while also tracking non-financial performance through environmental indicators. Although some green or impact funds may accept concessionary returns in exchange for high-impact outcomes, many seek to demonstrate that strong environmental results can be achieved without compromising financial performance.

Overall, integrating sustainability considerations into each phase of the fund lifecycle helps ensure that green investment funds meet both investor expectations and environmental objectives, reinforcing their role as effective tools within the sustainable finance landscape.

Chapter 5: Carbon Markets and Offsetting Mechanisms

Carbon markets and offsetting mechanisms are essential tools within the broader framework of green finance, enabling the pricing of greenhouse gas emissions and the channeling of capital toward emissions reduction projects. These mechanisms are designed to support cost-effective climate mitigation by allowing entities to meet targets through market-based approaches. This chapter explores the structure and function of both compliance and voluntary carbon markets, the development of offset credits, and the evolving standards and governance frameworks that underpin their credibility. It also examines challenges such as additionality, double-counting, and the role of offsets in supporting transition strategies.

Compliance vs. Voluntary Carbon Markets

Carbon markets operate through two primary frameworks: compliance markets and voluntary markets. While both aim to facilitate the reduction of GHG emissions, they differ significantly in terms of structure, participants, regulatory oversight, and intended use.

Compliance carbon markets are established and governed by legislation or regulation, typically as part of national, regional, or international climate policy frameworks. The most prominent example is the European Union Emissions Trading System (EU ETS), which sets a cap on total emissions allowed within specific sectors and allocates or auctions emissions allowances to covered entities. These entities must hold allowances equal to their actual emissions or face penalties. Allowances can be traded, creating a market price for carbon and incentivizing cost-effective abatement.

Other examples of compliance markets include the California Cap-and-Trade Program, the Regional Greenhouse Gas Initiative (RGGI) in the northeastern United States, and various emerging schemes in

Asia, such as China's national ETS. These systems are typically mandatory for large emitters in sectors like power generation, manufacturing, and aviation. Compliance markets are characterized by formal rules, government oversight, and robust monitoring, reporting, and verification (MRV) requirements.

In contrast, voluntary carbon markets allow organizations, companies, or individuals to purchase carbon credits on a discretionary basis to offset emissions or support climate action. These credits are generated from projects that reduce or remove emissions—such as reforestation, renewable energy installations, or methane capture—outside of regulated frameworks. Buyers may use credits to meet corporate climate targets, demonstrate environmental leadership, or prepare for future regulation.

Voluntary markets operate independently of government mandates but rely on voluntary standards, such as the Verified Carbon Standard (VCS), Gold Standard, and Climate Action Reserve, which set criteria for credit issuance, additionality, permanence, and third-party verification. Market infrastructure includes project developers, verifiers, registries, and brokers.

While compliance markets are policy-driven and enforceable, voluntary markets offer flexibility and innovation. However, they also face challenges, including inconsistent methodologies, concerns about credit quality, and limited price transparency. Recent efforts to improve integrity and scale include the formation of initiatives like the Integrity Council for the Voluntary Carbon Market (ICVCM) and the Voluntary Carbon Markets Integrity Initiative (VCMI).

Together, compliance and voluntary carbon markets provide mechanisms to put a price on carbon and incentivize emissions reductions. Their continued development is critical to supporting climate goals and mobilizing investment in mitigation across sectors and geographies.

Emissions Trading and Carbon Pricing

Carbon pricing is a policy approach that assigns a monetary value to GHG emissions, creating an economic incentive to reduce emissions and invest in low-carbon technologies. It is based on the principle that the costs of emitting carbon—such as climate change impacts—should be internalized by those responsible for the emissions. The two main forms of carbon pricing are emissions trading systems (ETS) and carbon taxes.

An emissions trading system, also known as a cap-and-trade program, sets a limit or cap on total emissions from regulated sectors. Under this model, allowances equal to the cap are distributed through free allocation or auction. Regulated entities are required to hold allowances equivalent to their actual emissions. Entities that reduce emissions below their allowance levels can sell excess allowances to others, while those exceeding their limits must purchase additional allowances. This creates a market price for carbon and encourages emitters to reduce emissions where it is most cost-effective.

The EU ETS is the most established example, covering power generation, industrial facilities, and aviation. It has served as a reference model for other jurisdictions implementing carbon markets, such as South Korea, China, New Zealand, and several subnational regions in North America. Design features—including allowance allocation, market stability mechanisms, and offset eligibility—vary across systems but share the common goal of delivering emissions reductions through market-based incentives.

Carbon taxes, in contrast, impose a fixed price on GHG emissions, usually expressed as a cost per metric ton of carbon dioxide equivalent (tCO_2e). Entities are taxed based on the amount of emissions they produce, regardless of their sector or size. Carbon taxes offer price certainty but do not guarantee a specific quantity of emissions reduction. They are simpler to administer than ETS and are often favored in jurisdictions with limited administrative capacity.

Some countries implement hybrid approaches that combine elements of both systems to balance price stability with environmental effectiveness. Carbon pricing revenues can be used to fund climate initiatives, support vulnerable communities, or reduce other taxes, depending on national priorities.

The effectiveness of carbon pricing depends on several factors, including the coverage of emissions sources, the level of the price or cap, and complementary policies. When well-designed, carbon pricing can shift investment flows toward cleaner technologies, drive innovation, and play a central role in national and international climate strategies.

As global momentum for climate action increases, emissions trading and carbon pricing continue to expand, providing governments and markets with flexible tools to reduce emissions efficiently and at scale.

Offsetting and Nature-Based Solutions

Carbon offsetting is a mechanism that allows entities to compensate for their GHG emissions by purchasing credits generated from projects that either reduce emissions elsewhere or remove carbon from the atmosphere. These credits, typically measured in metric tCO_2e, are used to balance out emissions that cannot be eliminated through direct mitigation. Offsetting is commonly applied within the voluntary carbon market but is also permitted under some compliance schemes with specific conditions.

A significant portion of carbon offsets is derived from nature-based solutions (NbS), which leverage natural systems to mitigate climate change while delivering additional environmental and social co-benefits. These solutions include activities such as reforestation, afforestation, avoided deforestation, wetland restoration, sustainable land management, and soil carbon sequestration. In addition to sequestering carbon, nature-based solutions contribute to biodiversity conservation, water regulation, and resilience to climate impacts.

Projects that generate offset credits from nature-based activities must meet specific standards to ensure environmental integrity and credibility. Key criteria include additionality (ensuring the project would not have occurred without carbon finance), permanence (ensuring carbon is stored for the long term), and leakage prevention (ensuring emissions are not displaced to other locations). Independent third-party verification and adherence to standards such as the VCS, Gold Standard, or Plan Vivo are essential to establish market confidence.

Nature-based offsetting has gained popularity as companies seek pathways to meet net-zero commitments. However, it has also attracted scrutiny due to concerns about the quality, permanence, and verifiability of certain projects. Issues such as over-crediting, underperformance, and insufficient monitoring have highlighted the need for robust governance frameworks and transparent reporting.

Recent initiatives, such as the LEAF Coalition and the ICVCM, aim to improve transparency, quality assurance, and alignment with global climate goals. These efforts seek to standardize methodologies, enhance oversight, and encourage the integration of nature-based solutions into national climate strategies, including nationally determined contributions (NDCs) under the Paris Agreement.

While offsetting through nature-based solutions should not replace direct emissions reductions, it can play a complementary role in overall climate strategies, particularly in hard-to-abate sectors. When used responsibly, offsetting enables capital to flow toward conservation and restoration projects that contribute to both climate mitigation and broader ecosystem services.

As the market evolves, integrating high-quality, nature-based offsets into green finance strategies can enhance environmental outcomes and support a more holistic approach to sustainability.

Credit Integrity and Additionality

Maintaining the integrity of carbon credits is essential to ensuring that offsetting mechanisms contribute meaningfully to climate mitigation efforts. Credit integrity refers to the accuracy, reliability, and environmental legitimacy of a carbon credit, while additionality is a core criterion that determines whether the emission reduction or removal would have occurred in the absence of carbon finance.

For a credit to be considered environmentally credible, it must represent a real, measurable, and verifiable reduction or removal of GHG emissions. This requires robust project design, transparent monitoring and reporting systems, and third-party verification. Standards bodies such as the VCS, Gold Standard, and Climate Action Reserve provide frameworks that establish methodologies for calculating emissions reductions and maintaining project transparency.

Additionality is a foundational principle in credit issuance. It ensures that projects are not receiving credits for outcomes that would have happened anyway due to existing policies, regulations, or market trends. For instance, if a renewable energy project is already economically viable without carbon financing, its emission reductions may not be considered additional. Failing to meet this standard risks undermining the environmental impact of offsetting and may lead to double counting of emissions reductions.

Assessing additionality involves a combination of financial, regulatory, and technical analyses. Project developers must demonstrate that carbon finance plays a decisive role in enabling the project. This is typically supported through documentation such as business-as-usual scenarios, financial modeling, and legal baselines.

Independent auditors review these assessments as part of the verification process.

Other factors contributing to credit integrity include permanence and leakage control. Permanence ensures that carbon sequestration, particularly in nature-based projects, is maintained over time and not reversed due to events such as deforestation, fire, or land-use change. Leakage control ensures that emissions reductions in one area do not lead to increases elsewhere, which would offset the environmental benefit.

The credibility of carbon markets depends on consistent application of these principles. In response to growing concerns, market actors are increasingly focused on improving transparency, governance, and standardization. Emerging initiatives aim to strengthen assurance frameworks and promote alignment with science-based climate targets.

Ensuring credit integrity and additionality is essential for building trust in offsetting mechanisms and for mobilizing capital toward projects that deliver genuine and lasting climate benefits.

International Frameworks (Paris Agreement Article 6)

Article 6 of the Paris Agreement establishes a framework for voluntary international cooperation in achieving climate goals through the use of market and non-market mechanisms. These provisions are designed to facilitate higher ambition in mitigation and adaptation actions, promote sustainable development, and ensure environmental integrity through transparent and accountable systems. Article 6 provides the basis for international carbon credit trading between countries and introduces formal structures that can enhance the credibility and impact of global carbon markets.

Article 6.2 allows countries to engage in bilateral or multilateral transfers of mitigation outcomes, known as Internationally Transferred Mitigation Outcomes (ITMOs). These transactions enable one country to finance emissions reductions in another and count them toward its own nationally determined contribution (NDC), provided proper accounting measures are followed. To avoid double counting, countries must apply corresponding adjustments—deducting emissions reductions from the host country's total and adding them to the acquiring country's total. This ensures the integrity of international cooperation and transparency in meeting climate commitments.

Article 6.4 establishes a centralized market mechanism overseen by a supervisory body under the United Nations Framework Convention on Climate Change (UNFCCC). This mechanism is designed to replace the Clean Development Mechanism (CDM) from the Kyoto Protocol and aims to facilitate the generation and transfer of verified emissions reductions through registered projects and programs. The Article 6.4 mechanism includes provisions for stakeholder participation, sustainable development benefits, and robust monitoring and verification systems.

Article 6.8, in contrast, focuses on non-market approaches, such as climate finance, technology transfer, and capacity-building activities. These are intended to complement market mechanisms and ensure a more inclusive and diversified pathway for countries to achieve their NDCs, particularly those with limited access to carbon market infrastructure.

Operationalizing Article 6 has been a complex and iterative process, requiring extensive negotiations on accounting rules, transparency requirements, and governance structures. The rules adopted at COP26 in Glasgow (2021) and refined at subsequent conferences represent a significant step toward enabling international carbon cooperation while maintaining environmental integrity.

As Article 6 mechanisms become more operational, they are expected to reshape global carbon markets, offering new channels for public and private finance to support emissions reductions across borders. Their success will depend on consistent implementation, strong oversight, and the ability to link national climate ambition with credible mitigation outcomes.

Challenges and Emerging Trends

As carbon markets and offsetting mechanisms continue to evolve, they face several challenges that may affect their credibility, scalability, and long-term role in global climate strategies. At the same time, new trends are emerging that aim to strengthen the integrity, effectiveness, and integration of these tools within broader green finance frameworks.

One of the central challenges is ensuring the environmental integrity of carbon credits. Concerns persist about the additionality, permanence, and verification of projects, particularly in the voluntary carbon market. Instances of over-crediting, inconsistent methodologies, and insufficient monitoring have prompted scrutiny from stakeholders and regulators. Addressing these issues requires robust standards, independent oversight, and continuous improvements in measurement, reporting, and verification (MRV) systems.

Another challenge is the risk of double counting, especially in international markets where the same emissions reduction may be claimed by multiple parties—such as a host country and a credit buyer. The implementation of corresponding adjustments under Article 6 of the Paris Agreement aims to resolve this issue, but ensuring compliance and consistency across jurisdictions remains complex.

Market fragmentation also poses a barrier to scaling up carbon trading. Numerous registries, standards, and trading platforms operate independently, leading to lack of coordination and varying definitions of credit quality. Efforts to harmonize market practices and enhance transparency are underway through initiatives such as the ICVCM and the VCMI.

In response to these challenges, several emerging trends are shaping the future of carbon markets. One such trend is the integration of digital technologies, including blockchain and satellite monitoring, to improve traceability, reduce transaction costs, and enhance data accuracy. These innovations can support more efficient credit issuance and verification processes.

There is also increasing attention on co-benefits and just transitions, with stakeholders emphasizing the importance of delivering social and biodiversity outcomes alongside emissions reductions. Projects that incorporate safeguards for local communities, indigenous rights, and ecosystem protection are gaining traction among investors and buyers seeking high-quality, ethical offsets.

Additionally, corporate climate strategies are evolving, with a growing emphasis on reducing absolute emissions before relying on offsets. This is leading to clearer offsetting hierarchies and net-zero alignment standards that differentiate between reduction and removal credits.

Overall, overcoming challenges and embracing emerging trends will be essential to building carbon markets that are transparent, credible, and aligned with long-term climate goals.

Chapter 6: Guarantees, Insurance, and Risk-Sharing Mechanisms

Guarantees, insurance products, and risk-sharing mechanisms are essential tools within green finance, helping to mobilize investment by mitigating financial, political, and technical risks associated with environmentally sustainable projects. These instruments are particularly relevant in emerging and developing markets, where perceived or actual risks can limit private sector participation. By improving creditworthiness, reducing uncertainty, and enhancing project bankability, risk mitigation tools play a catalytic role in scaling up green investment. This chapter explores the structure, function, and application of guarantees and insurance instruments, with attention to their role in de-risking green projects and supporting blended finance strategies.

The Role of Risk Mitigation in Green Finance

Risk mitigation plays a critical role in mobilizing capital for green finance by addressing the financial, political, and operational uncertainties that often accompany environmentally sustainable investments. Green projects—such as renewable energy infrastructure, energy efficiency upgrades, or climate resilience initiatives—may involve long payback periods, technology risks, evolving regulatory environments, or market volatility. These characteristics can deter private sector participation, particularly in markets perceived as high-risk.

Risk mitigation tools such as guarantees, insurance products, and structured risk-sharing arrangements are designed to reduce the exposure of investors and lenders to these uncertainties. By improving the risk-return profile of green projects, these instruments help unlock financing that might not otherwise be available under standard commercial terms.

In green finance, risk mitigation is particularly important for enabling blended finance structures, where concessional or public finance is used alongside private capital. In such arrangements, guarantees and insurance products serve to reduce the risk borne by private investors, making it more attractive for them to support projects that deliver environmental benefits. This can be especially impactful in low- and middle-income countries, where access to affordable long-term finance is limited and green investment opportunities may be perceived as untested or high-risk.

Risk mitigation also supports financial innovation by enabling new types of investment vehicles or financing models. For example, credit guarantees can facilitate the issuance of green bonds by improving the credit rating of the issuer or underlying assets. Political risk insurance can protect against changes in government policy that affect renewable energy tariffs or land use permissions.

DFIs, MDBs, and export credit agencies are key providers of risk mitigation instruments in the green finance landscape. Their participation enhances confidence in project bankability and often acts as a signal to other market participants.

As green finance continues to expand, effective risk mitigation will remain a cornerstone for attracting diverse sources of capital. Designing tailored, transparent, and accessible risk mitigation tools can help accelerate the deployment of green solutions, particularly in sectors or regions where private investment is constrained by real or perceived risks.

Green Credit Guarantees

Green credit guarantees are financial instruments that provide partial or full assurance to lenders or investors that they will be compensated in the event of borrower default. In the context of green finance, these guarantees are specifically applied to loans or investments supporting environmentally sustainable projects, such as renewable energy, energy efficiency, sustainable agriculture, or climate adaptation initiatives.

The primary function of a green credit guarantee is to enhance creditworthiness and reduce the perceived risk of lending to green projects or borrowers that may not meet conventional credit criteria. By shifting a portion of the default risk from the lender to the guarantor, these instruments facilitate access to finance for projects that are aligned with environmental objectives but may face barriers such as limited collateral, high upfront costs, or uncertain revenue streams.

Credit guarantees are particularly effective in mobilizing private capital for green projects in emerging markets or underserved sectors. In these contexts, local financial institutions may be unfamiliar with the risk-return profiles of green investments or lack the capacity to evaluate technical aspects. A guarantee can serve as a confidence-building mechanism, enabling lenders to extend credit to new types of projects or client segments.

Green credit guarantees may be provided by a variety of actors, including DFIs, MDBs, national development banks, and in some cases, specialized green guarantee facilities. These entities often design guarantee schemes to align with broader policy goals, such as supporting clean energy deployment, promoting climate-resilient infrastructure, or advancing green SMEs.

Guarantee structures vary widely but often include a partial credit guarantee, where the guarantor covers a fixed percentage of the loan principal in case of default. This approach ensures that the lender retains some exposure, maintaining incentives for sound credit assessment. In other cases, full guarantees may be offered for strategic or demonstration purposes, particularly in early-stage market development.

In addition to reducing credit risk, guarantees can help borrowers secure better loan terms, including lower interest rates, longer tenors, or reduced collateral requirements. This can improve the financial viability of green projects and expand access to finance for organizations with limited borrowing capacity.

To maximize impact, guarantee programs often incorporate technical assistance components, supporting both lenders and borrowers in project design, environmental due diligence, and compliance with sustainability standards.

Overall, green credit guarantees are a valuable tool for de-risking investment, encouraging financial inclusion, and scaling up capital flows toward climate and environmental goals.

Climate Risk Insurance Tools

Climate risk insurance tools are financial instruments designed to protect individuals, businesses, and governments against the economic impacts of climate-related hazards. These tools provide compensation or financial relief in the event of extreme weather events or slow-onset climate impacts, such as floods, droughts, storms, or sea-level rise. By transferring risk from vulnerable stakeholders to insurers, climate risk insurance contributes to climate resilience and supports broader green finance objectives.

These insurance mechanisms can be categorized into two broad types: indemnity-based insurance and parametric insurance. Indemnity-based insurance compensates for actual losses incurred, following an assessment of the damage. This traditional approach is commonly used in agriculture, property, and infrastructure sectors. In contrast, parametric insurance pays out a predetermined amount based on the occurrence of a specified event—such as rainfall below a certain threshold or wind speed exceeding a defined level—regardless of actual losses. Parametric insurance offers faster payouts and lower administrative costs, making it well-suited for addressing climate shocks in remote or underserved areas.

Climate risk insurance plays a critical role in de-risking green investments, especially in sectors like renewable energy, sustainable agriculture, or water infrastructure. For example, solar and wind power projects are exposed to weather variability that can affect energy generation and revenue stability. Insurance products that cover resource volatility can enhance the bankability of such projects and attract private capital.

Governments and international institutions often support climate insurance schemes through public-private partnerships. These arrangements may include premium subsidies, reinsurance facilities, or the establishment of regional risk pools. Examples include the African Risk Capacity (ARC), the Caribbean Catastrophe Risk Insurance Facility (CCRIF), and the Pacific Catastrophe Risk Assessment and Financing Initiative (PCRAFI). Such programs help spread risk across countries and provide access to capital in the aftermath of disasters.

At the micro level, index-based insurance has been developed for smallholder farmers and vulnerable communities, offering protection against crop failure due to climate extremes. These products support livelihoods and promote investment in sustainable practices by reducing the financial burden of climate-related losses.

Climate risk insurance also contributes to financial system stability by reducing the exposure of lenders and investors to uninsured climate impacts. As climate risks become more material to portfolios, insurers are working with financial institutions to integrate risk modeling, promote risk awareness, and develop innovative insurance-linked securities.

Overall, climate risk insurance tools are essential for enhancing climate resilience, managing financial risk, and enabling the expansion of sustainable investment in a changing climate.

Role of International Agencies (e.g., MIGA, GCF)

International agencies play a central role in supporting risk mitigation within green finance by providing financial instruments, technical assistance, and policy support to help de-risk environmentally sustainable investments. Organizations such as the Multilateral Investment Guarantee Agency (MIGA) and the Green Climate Fund (GCF) are instrumental in enabling capital flows to projects that align with climate goals but may face market, political, or institutional barriers.

MIGA, a member of the World Bank Group, offers political risk insurance and credit enhancement products to investors and lenders in developing countries. Its guarantees cover risks such as expropriation, breach of contract, currency inconvertibility, and civil disturbance—risks that can deter private sector participation in green infrastructure, renewable energy, or climate adaptation initiatives. By mitigating these risks, MIGA helps improve the bankability of projects and attract foreign direct investment to climate-aligned sectors in emerging economies.

The Green Climate Fund, established under the UNFCCC, provides concessional finance, risk-sharing instruments, and grants to support climate mitigation and adaptation efforts in developing countries. The GCF works through a network of accredited entities, including development banks, commercial financial institutions, and non-governmental organizations. Through its financial instruments—such as first-loss equity, guarantees, and subordinated debt—the GCF helps crowd in private capital and promote investment in early-stage or high-risk green initiatives.

Both MIGA and GCF also contribute to the development of financial frameworks and project pipelines, offering capacity-building support, stakeholder engagement, and safeguards that align projects with international environmental and social standards. These services are particularly valuable in regions with limited institutional capacity or where climate finance markets are still emerging.

In addition to MIGA and GCF, other international agencies such as the International Finance Corporation (IFC), the EIB, and various regional development banks offer complementary risk mitigation tools. These may include partial credit guarantees, technical assistance, or blended finance structures designed to lower barriers to entry for sustainable investments.

The involvement of international agencies enhances market confidence, reduces transaction costs, and helps structure deals that might not otherwise proceed. Their ability to absorb or share risk, combined with their convening power and technical expertise, makes them vital actors in the global effort to mobilize finance for climate and environmental goals.

Contingent Finance and Disaster Risk

Contingent finance refers to pre-arranged financial instruments that provide rapid access to funding in response to predefined triggers, such as natural disasters or climate-related shocks. In the context of green finance, contingent finance mechanisms are increasingly used to manage disaster risk and support the resilience of vulnerable countries, regions, and sectors. These tools are designed to improve preparedness, reduce recovery time, and limit the long-term economic and social impacts of extreme events.

One of the most common forms of contingent finance is the catastrophe-contingent credit line, which disburses funds when a natural disaster—such as a flood, cyclone, drought, or earthquake—occurs and meets predefined parameters. These credit lines are typically offered by MDBs, such as the World Bank's Catastrophe Deferred Drawdown Option (Cat-DDO), and are intended to complement broader disaster risk management strategies.

Another mechanism is parametric insurance-linked finance, which releases funding based on specific environmental or physical triggers, such as rainfall levels, wind speeds, or seismic activity. This approach ensures rapid disbursement of funds, often within days, which is critical for early response and recovery efforts. Unlike traditional indemnity-based financing, parametric mechanisms do not require a detailed loss assessment, reducing administrative delays and uncertainty.

Contingent finance is particularly valuable for climate-vulnerable countries that face fiscal constraints and high exposure to climate risks. It enables governments to plan for emergency response without diverting funds from long-term development priorities. Additionally, these tools help attract private investment by demonstrating that climate-related risks are being proactively managed through financial planning and resilience measures.

The integration of contingent finance into national climate adaptation and disaster risk reduction strategies is supported by development partners, regional risk pools, and international climate finance mechanisms. Examples include the CCRIF and the ARC, which provide pooled insurance coverage supported by contingent credit.

While contingent finance cannot eliminate the physical risks associated with climate change, it can play a critical role in enhancing financial preparedness, supporting recovery, and maintaining macroeconomic stability. As climate-related hazards increase in frequency and severity, contingent finance will remain an important component of climate-resilient financial planning.

Leveraging Guarantees to Mobilize Private Capital

Guarantees are a key risk mitigation tool that can be strategically used to mobilize private capital into green sectors by reducing the financial risk exposure of investors and lenders. In green finance, guarantees help bridge the gap between risk-averse private actors and the perceived uncertainty associated with sustainable or climate-related investments. This is especially relevant in emerging markets or in sectors characterized by long project horizons, new technologies, or regulatory complexity.

Guarantees function by offering partial or full protection against specific risks—such as credit default, political instability, or foreign exchange fluctuations—thereby enhancing the risk-return profile of a given transaction. For private investors, this reassurance can unlock investments that might otherwise be considered too risky or unbankable. Guarantees can also lower the cost of capital by improving borrower creditworthiness or enabling better financing terms.

DFIs, MDBs, and specialized guarantee facilities often take the lead in offering guarantees to support green investments. These entities can assume risks that private actors are unwilling to bear, acting as first-loss providers or co-guarantors. Their involvement can crowd in private finance by signaling that projects meet established due diligence and environmental standards.

Guarantees are also frequently embedded in blended finance structures, where public or concessional capital is combined with commercial investment. In such arrangements, guarantees can be used to absorb early losses, backstop payment obligations, or ensure coverage of specific risk layers. This flexibility makes them adaptable to a wide range of financing structures, from loans and bonds to equity investments.

Examples of successful applications include guarantees that support green bond issuances by improving credit ratings, thereby attracting a broader base of institutional investors. Similarly, guarantees for off-grid renewable energy projects can mitigate payment default risks from local utilities or small-scale customers, helping to scale energy access in underserved areas.

While guarantees are not a standalone solution, they are an effective catalytic instrument when used strategically as part of broader investment frameworks. The key to their effectiveness lies in careful design, transparent governance, and alignment with both environmental and financial objectives.

As demand for climate finance grows, leveraging guarantees to mobilize private capital will remain an essential strategy for accelerating the deployment of sustainable infrastructure and scaling climate-aligned investment globally.

Chapter 7: Taxonomies, Standards, and Disclosure Tools

As green finance continues to expand, the need for clarity, consistency, and transparency has led to the development of taxonomies, reporting standards, and disclosure tools. These frameworks provide the foundation for defining what constitutes environmentally sustainable activities, assessing alignment with climate goals, and informing investment decisions. They are also essential for managing greenwashing risks and ensuring comparability across financial products and markets. This chapter explores the role of green taxonomies, sustainability reporting frameworks, and environmental performance metrics in supporting the credibility and effectiveness of green finance.

What Are Green Taxonomies?

Green taxonomies are classification systems that define which economic activities can be considered environmentally sustainable. Their primary purpose is to create a common understanding of what qualifies as "green," helping investors, financial institutions, policymakers, and companies align capital flows with environmental and climate goals. By providing a clear set of criteria, taxonomies contribute to greater consistency, transparency, and accountability in green finance.

At their core, green taxonomies set out technical screening criteria that determine whether an activity contributes substantially to one or more environmental objectives, such as climate change mitigation, climate change adaptation, pollution prevention, sustainable water use, circular economy, or biodiversity protection. In many cases, taxonomies also include do no significant harm (DNSH) safeguards, which require that the activity does not adversely impact other environmental goals. Additionally, minimum social safeguards may be included to ensure alignment with international labor and human rights standards.

The development of green taxonomies is often led by national governments, regional blocs, or international organizations. One of the most influential examples is the European Union (EU) Taxonomy, which serves as a regulatory framework for classifying sustainable economic activities within the EU's financial system. Other countries and regions—including China, Colombia, South Africa, and the Association of Southeast Asian Nations (ASEAN)—have developed or are in the process of developing their own taxonomies, often tailored to local economic structures and policy priorities.

Green taxonomies are used by a variety of stakeholders. Investors use them to identify eligible assets for green portfolios. Financial institutions apply taxonomy criteria in sustainable lending, bond issuance, or risk assessment processes. Corporates use taxonomies for sustainability reporting, strategy development, and regulatory compliance. Policymakers and regulators rely on taxonomies to design incentive schemes, guide public spending, and monitor market alignment with environmental goals.

While green taxonomies enhance market clarity, they also present challenges related to implementation, comparability, and data availability. Differences between national taxonomies can lead to fragmentation, and the evolving nature of screening criteria may create uncertainty for market participants.

Nevertheless, green taxonomies are becoming a cornerstone of sustainable finance infrastructure. They provide a shared language for identifying and scaling investments that support environmental objectives, helping to build a more credible and effective green finance ecosystem.

Global Taxonomy Landscape (EU, China, ASEAN, etc.)

The development of green taxonomies has become a global priority as jurisdictions seek to channel investment toward sustainable economic activities and meet environmental and climate targets. While many taxonomies share similar goals—such as enhancing transparency, reducing greenwashing, and aligning finance with national or international commitments—they differ in structure, scope, and application based on local policy contexts and market needs.

The EU Taxonomy is one of the most advanced and comprehensive frameworks to date. Introduced under the EU Sustainable Finance Action Plan, it provides a science-based classification system covering six environmental objectives, including climate change mitigation and adaptation. The EU Taxonomy establishes technical screening criteria, minimum social safeguards, and "do no significant harm" (DNSH) principles. It is mandatory for certain financial market participants, corporates, and public entities in the EU to disclose the alignment of their activities with the taxonomy, supporting comparability across investments and disclosures.

China has developed its own Green Bond Endorsed Project Catalogue, which serves as a de facto taxonomy for the green bond market. Historically, China's taxonomy differed from others by including certain transitional activities, such as clean coal. However, in recent years, efforts have been made to bring it closer in line with international practices. In 2021, China and the EU launched the Common Ground Taxonomy (CGT) initiative through the International Platform on Sustainable Finance (IPSF) to identify areas of convergence and promote interoperability between systems.

The Association of Southeast Asian Nations (ASEAN) released the ASEAN Taxonomy for Sustainable Finance, aimed at providing a common framework for member states while allowing for national flexibility. The taxonomy includes a tiered approach to classification, reflecting the varied levels of development and environmental policy frameworks across the region. It supports both climate mitigation and adaptation goals and encourages progressive improvement over time.

Other countries, including South Africa, Colombia, and the United Kingdom, are developing or implementing their own green taxonomies, often building on the structure of the EU Taxonomy or adapting it to their local context. These efforts reflect a broader trend toward formalizing sustainable finance frameworks within regulatory systems.

Despite growing interest and adoption, the lack of harmonization remains a challenge. Divergences in definitions, thresholds, and methodologies can hinder cross-border investment and increase compliance complexity. Initiatives such as the IPSF and ongoing international dialogues aim to promote greater interoperability and mutual recognition of taxonomies.

As taxonomies continue to evolve, global coordination and alignment will be essential to ensuring that these tools support a coherent and efficient transition to a more sustainable global economy.

ESG Disclosure Standards (TCFD, ISSB, SFDR)

ESG disclosure standards are critical to enhancing transparency, comparability, and accountability in sustainable finance. As the demand for consistent and decision-useful sustainability information grows, a number of global and regional frameworks have been developed to guide how companies and financial institutions disclose ESG-related data. Among the most widely recognized standards are the Task Force on Climate-related Financial Disclosures (TCFD), the International Sustainability Standards Board (ISSB) framework, and the SFDR in the European Union.

The TCFD, established by the Financial Stability Board, provides a voluntary framework for climate-related financial disclosures. It recommends that organizations disclose information across four key areas: governance, strategy, risk management, and metrics and targets. The goal is to help investors and other stakeholders assess how climate-related risks and opportunities could affect an organization's financial performance. TCFD has gained global traction and is increasingly being adopted or mandated by regulators in jurisdictions such as the United Kingdom, Japan, New Zealand, and Canada.

Building on the TCFD framework, the ISSB was created by the International Financial Reporting Standards (IFRS) Foundation to consolidate and streamline sustainability disclosure standards globally. In 2023, the ISSB released its first two standards—IFRS S1 on general sustainability-related disclosures and IFRS S2 on climate-related disclosures. These standards aim to create a consistent baseline for global reporting, allowing investors to compare sustainability performance across sectors and jurisdictions. The ISSB framework is expected to play a central role in aligning reporting requirements and reducing fragmentation in ESG disclosures.

The SFDR, by contrast, is a regulatory framework specific to the European Union. It requires financial market participants—including asset managers, insurers, and pension funds—to disclose how they integrate ESG risks and sustainability considerations into investment decisions and financial products. The SFDR introduces product classification (Articles 6, 8, and 9) to distinguish between products based on their sustainability profile, with corresponding disclosure obligations. It also requires reporting on principal adverse impacts (PAIs) on sustainability factors.

While these frameworks serve different purposes and operate at different levels—TCFD and ISSB at the corporate reporting level, SFDR at the financial product level—they are interrelated and increasingly complementary. Many institutions use TCFD-aligned reporting to meet ISSB requirements, and SFDR disclosures often rely on underlying corporate sustainability data.

As ESG disclosure standards continue to evolve, convergence and interoperability remain important to reducing reporting burdens, improving data quality, and supporting the integrity of sustainable finance markets globally.

Performance Metrics and Impact Measurement

Performance metrics and impact measurement are essential components of green finance, enabling stakeholders to assess the effectiveness of investments in achieving environmental objectives. These tools provide the basis for monitoring progress, demonstrating accountability, and guiding decision-making. As sustainable finance grows, the demand for reliable, consistent, and comparable data on environmental performance continues to increase across public and private sectors.

Performance metrics refer to quantitative indicators used to evaluate the environmental outcomes of an investment or activity. These metrics may capture a range of sustainability dimensions, such as GHG emissions reductions, energy efficiency gains, renewable energy capacity installed, water savings, waste diverted from landfills, or improvements in biodiversity. The selection of appropriate metrics depends on the nature of the activity, sector, and intended impact, as well as the reporting requirements of relevant frameworks or investors.

To support comparability and standardization, organizations often align with existing impact measurement frameworks. Prominent examples include the Global Impact Investing Network's (GIIN) IRIS+ system, which offers standardized indicators for various sectors and outcomes, and the Impact Management Platform, which promotes coherence among impact measurement approaches. In addition, the Partnership for Carbon Accounting Financials (PCAF) provides methodologies for financial institutions to measure and disclose financed emissions.

Performance metrics are also increasingly integrated into reporting standards and regulatory frameworks. For example, under the European Union's SFDR, financial market participants must report on indicators such as carbon footprint and exposure to fossil fuels. Similarly, the ISSB encourages the use of decision-useful metrics to inform investor assessments.

Impact measurement goes beyond performance tracking by assessing whether the intended environmental changes have occurred and can be attributed to the financed activity. This process may include setting baselines, defining targets, and applying methodologies to determine causality. While attribution can be complex, especially in multi-stakeholder environments, transparent methodologies and independent verification can help strengthen confidence in reported outcomes.

Challenges in performance measurement include data availability, methodological consistency, and verification capacity. As a result, continuous improvement in data systems, digital tools, and capacity building is needed to enhance the quality and utility of environmental metrics.

Ultimately, robust performance metrics and impact measurement are foundational to the credibility and effectiveness of green finance. They support transparency, enable informed investment decisions, and contribute to aligning financial flows with environmental and climate goals.

Role of Digital Platforms and ESG Data

Digital platforms and ESG data play an increasingly important role in supporting transparency, comparability, and decision-making in green finance. As demand for sustainability-related information grows, digital technologies are enhancing the way ESG data is collected, processed, analyzed, and reported across financial markets. These advancements are contributing to the development of more efficient, accurate, and accessible green finance systems.

Digital platforms serve as centralized hubs for ESG data management, enabling issuers, investors, and regulators to interact with sustainability information in real time. These platforms support data integration from multiple sources, including corporate disclosures, satellite imagery, supply chain data, and climate risk models. They also facilitate automated reporting, performance tracking, and benchmarking, reducing the administrative burden on organizations while improving data consistency and timeliness.

ESG data providers—both established firms and emerging fintech companies—are leveraging digital tools such as artificial intelligence (AI), machine learning, and natural language processing to extract and standardize non-financial information from various sources. These technologies help interpret large volumes of sustainability data, identify trends, and detect inconsistencies, offering deeper insights into company practices and portfolio risks.

Digital platforms are also playing a key role in green bond and sustainable finance registries, where they provide searchable databases of issuances, project categories, and impact metrics. By aggregating and publishing information in standardized formats, these platforms enhance market transparency and support investor due diligence.

Another area of growth is in climate and ESG data analytics, which help financial institutions assess exposure to physical and transition risks, forecast sustainability performance, and model climate-aligned investment scenarios. These analytics tools are often integrated into investment platforms, enabling users to assess ESG risks and opportunities alongside traditional financial metrics.

Despite these advancements, challenges remain, particularly regarding data quality, interoperability, and transparency of methodologies used by ESG data providers. Inconsistent reporting standards, variations in data coverage, and limited verification can hinder the reliability of ESG assessments. Efforts to improve data governance, standardization, and digital infrastructure are ongoing through collaborative initiatives involving regulators, industry groups, and international organizations.

Overall, digital platforms and ESG data technologies are reshaping how green finance operates, providing the tools needed to manage sustainability information at scale. As these tools continue to evolve, they will play a critical role in supporting informed decision-making, market integrity, and alignment with long-term environmental objectives.

Regulation and Risk Management

The integration of ESG considerations into financial regulation and risk management frameworks is becoming a key component of sustainable finance. As climate-related and environmental risks increasingly affect economic stability and financial performance, regulators and financial institutions are incorporating sustainability factors into their supervisory practices, disclosure requirements, and risk assessment tools.

Regulatory authorities are recognizing that climate-related risks—including both physical risks from extreme weather events and transition risks from policy or market shifts—can pose material threats to financial systems. In response, central banks, financial regulators, and supervisory bodies are beginning to embed ESG and climate risks into existing prudential frameworks. These efforts aim to enhance the resilience of financial institutions and support the broader alignment of financial flows with climate and environmental objectives.

One of the key developments in this space is the adoption of climate-related stress testing and scenario analysis. Financial institutions are increasingly required or encouraged to assess how their portfolios would perform under different climate pathways, including scenarios consistent with net-zero transitions or higher global warming outcomes. These tools help institutions understand potential exposures and develop strategies to manage long-term risks.

Regulatory frameworks such as the EU SFDR and the EU Taxonomy Regulation mandate financial actors to disclose how they account for sustainability risks in their decision-making processes. Similar developments are underway in other jurisdictions, supported by global coordination efforts through initiatives like the Network for Greening the Financial System (NGFS) and the Financial Stability Board (FSB).

In parallel, financial institutions are integrating ESG factors into their internal risk management systems, including credit risk, market risk, and operational risk assessments. This involves incorporating ESG metrics into underwriting, due diligence, and investment processes, as well as updating governance structures and staff training to reflect sustainability priorities.

Despite progress, challenges persist, particularly in standardizing methodologies, ensuring access to high-quality data, and aligning regulatory approaches across jurisdictions. The dynamic nature of ESG risks also requires ongoing adaptation and capacity-building within both regulatory institutions and market participants.

Overall, integrating sustainability considerations into regulation and risk management is essential for promoting financial stability, improving transparency, and enabling the financial system to contribute meaningfully to environmental and climate objectives.

Chapter 8: Public Finance and Blended Finance Tools

Public finance and blended finance tools play a critical role in catalyzing investment in environmentally sustainable activities, particularly in markets or sectors where private capital alone may be insufficient. Public finance—including grants, concessional loans, and subsidies—helps address market failures and supports early-stage or high-risk green initiatives. Blended finance, by combining public and private capital, enables risk-sharing arrangements that can unlock additional investment at scale. This chapter explores the structure, function, and application of these tools, highlighting their role in advancing climate and environmental objectives across different financing contexts.

Public Sector Role in Green Finance

The public sector plays a foundational role in the development and expansion of green finance by creating enabling conditions, providing direct financial support, and guiding capital toward environmentally sustainable activities. Public sector institutions—including national governments, development banks, and multilateral agencies—contribute to green finance through a combination of policy instruments, public funding, and institutional frameworks.

One of the most significant contributions of the public sector is the development of regulatory and policy frameworks that establish clear signals and incentives for sustainable investment. These frameworks include environmental standards, carbon pricing mechanisms, renewable energy mandates, and climate-related disclosure requirements. By setting clear long-term objectives and reducing uncertainty, public policy can influence investor behavior and support the alignment of financial markets with climate and environmental goals.

In addition to policy measures, public sector entities provide direct financial support for green projects through grants, concessional loans, equity investments, and guarantees. These forms of capital are often critical in the early stages of project development, especially for high-impact but high-risk initiatives. Public finance can help cover transaction costs, support feasibility studies, and improve project bankability, particularly in sectors or regions where private investment is limited.

The public sector also facilitates the development of green financial infrastructure, including data platforms, taxonomies, sustainability standards, and technical assistance facilities. These resources enhance transparency, comparability, and credibility in green finance markets, supporting both public and private actors in their decision-making.

DFIs and national development banks often act as intermediaries, channeling public funds into strategic green sectors such as clean energy, sustainable transport, and climate adaptation. Their participation often signals project quality and aligns investment with broader development objectives.

Furthermore, public finance can play a countercyclical role, maintaining investment flows during periods of economic uncertainty or market disruption. This is particularly important for ensuring continuity in climate-aligned infrastructure development and for building resilience against environmental shocks.

By de-risking investments, setting standards, and mobilizing complementary private capital, the public sector remains a key driver in scaling up green finance. Its ability to integrate environmental considerations into fiscal planning and capital allocation strategies will continue to shape the trajectory of sustainable development globally.

Green Public Procurement and Budgeting

Green public procurement (GPP) and green budgeting are key policy tools that enable governments to integrate environmental objectives into fiscal decision-making and public expenditure. Through these instruments, the public sector can influence market behavior, promote sustainable production and consumption, and ensure that public resources are aligned with climate and environmental priorities.

Green public procurement involves the use of environmental criteria in the purchasing decisions of public authorities. It covers a wide range of goods, services, and infrastructure—such as energy-efficient buildings, low-emission vehicles, sustainable construction materials, and eco-labeled products. By embedding environmental considerations into procurement policies and tenders, governments can stimulate demand for greener solutions and support innovation in sustainable technologies.

The adoption of GPP can also lead to cost savings over the life cycle of products and services, as energy efficiency, durability, and reduced maintenance contribute to lower total costs. In addition, GPP helps set benchmarks for environmental performance and sends clear signals to suppliers about shifting market expectations. As one of the largest buyers in most economies, the public sector can use its purchasing power to accelerate the transition to more sustainable business practices.

To be effective, GPP requires a clear policy framework, robust criteria, and the capacity to evaluate environmental impacts throughout the procurement process. International initiatives, such as those led by the OECD and UNEP, have supported governments in developing guidelines and sharing best practices.

Green budgeting, meanwhile, refers to the integration of environmental and climate-related considerations into public financial management. It includes the assessment of how budgetary allocations, tax policies, and public investments affect environmental outcomes. Green budgeting can take various forms, including climate budget tagging, environmental expenditure reviews, and impact assessments of budget measures on emissions and natural resources.

This approach enables governments to track the environmental orientation of their budgets and align spending with national sustainability strategies, such as nationally determined contributions (NDCs) under the Paris Agreement. Green budgeting also enhances transparency and accountability by making environmental priorities visible in the budgeting process.

Several countries have begun implementing green budgeting frameworks, supported by multilateral organizations such as the IMF, World Bank, and OECD. These efforts contribute to building climate-resilient public finance systems and improving the alignment of fiscal policy with long-term sustainability goals.

Together, green public procurement and budgeting form an integrated approach to greening public finance. By leveraging both spending and policy instruments, governments can support the development of sustainable markets, enhance environmental outcomes, and lead by example in the transition to a low-carbon economy.

Green Investment Banks and DFIs

Green investment banks and DFIs play a pivotal role in financing environmentally sustainable projects by addressing market gaps, reducing perceived risks, and mobilizing private sector participation. These institutions are designed to support the scaling of green finance by providing targeted financial products, technical expertise, and long-term capital to projects that align with national and international climate and environmental objectives.

Green investment banks are typically public or quasi-public entities established to accelerate investment in clean energy, energy efficiency, sustainable transport, and climate resilience. Their mandates often focus on crowding in private capital by de-risking investments through instruments such as concessional loans, guarantees, subordinated debt, and equity co-investments. These banks may also provide project development assistance, support for green bond issuance, and tools for measuring environmental impact.

Examples of green investment banks include the UK Green Investment Bank (now part of the Green Investment Group), Australia's Clean Energy Finance Corporation (CEFC), and New York's Green Bank. These institutions have demonstrated the ability to leverage limited public capital to mobilize significantly larger amounts of private investment, often at favorable terms.

DFIs—which include both bilateral and multilateral entities—also play a major role in green finance, particularly in developing and emerging economies. DFIs such as the IFC, Asian Development Bank (ADB), and African Development Bank (AfDB) provide long-term financing and risk mitigation tools for projects that align with SDGs and climate strategies.

DFIs often act as anchor investors in green infrastructure and clean energy projects, helping to build confidence among commercial financiers. They also support capacity building, regulatory reforms, and market development to create enabling environments for sustainable investment. Many DFIs have adopted climate finance targets, established internal environmental and social safeguards, and developed sector-specific strategies to guide green investment.

In addition to direct financing, both green investment banks and DFIs contribute to knowledge sharing and innovation. By piloting new financing models, aggregating smaller-scale projects, and supporting blended finance structures, these institutions play a catalytic role in scaling up solutions that may otherwise face barriers to market entry.

While their approaches vary, green investment banks and DFIs are aligned in their goal of increasing the volume and impact of finance directed toward climate and environmental priorities. As global efforts to meet net-zero and sustainability targets intensify, these institutions will continue to be key enablers of the transition to a greener and more resilient economy.

Blended Finance Structures

Blended finance structures are designed to strategically use concessional public or philanthropic capital to mobilize private investment for projects with measurable development or environmental impact. These structures address market barriers by improving the risk-return profile of green investments, particularly in sectors, regions, or project stages where private capital may be reluctant to engage on purely commercial terms.

Blended finance typically combines different types of capital, each with distinct objectives and risk appetites. Public and concessional sources, such as DFIs, MDBs, or climate funds, provide risk-absorbing layers that can take the form of subordinated equity, first-loss guarantees, or interest rate subsidies. These elements are designed to protect commercial investors against specific risks—such as early-stage losses, political instability, or revenue variability—thereby creating incentives for private sector participation.

At the core of blended finance is the principle of additionality—the notion that concessional capital should only be used where it leads to additional private investment that would not otherwise occur. To achieve this, blended structures are carefully tailored based on project needs, sector dynamics, and investor expectations. Common applications include renewable energy infrastructure, climate-resilient agriculture, sustainable transport, and urban adaptation initiatives.

A typical blended finance structure might include a tiered capital stack, with public capital assuming the highest-risk tranche, followed by mezzanine and senior tranches held by private investors. This approach allows for risk-sharing and can improve financing terms such as tenor, pricing, and collateral requirements. Blended structures may also include technical assistance components to strengthen project design, build local capacity, or support compliance with environmental and social safeguards.

Blended finance is often facilitated through specialized platforms or investment vehicles, including green funds, project preparation facilities, or climate-focused development initiatives. These entities coordinate capital contributions, manage due diligence, and ensure alignment with environmental objectives and performance metrics.

Challenges in blended finance include ensuring transparency in concessionality, avoiding market distortion, and setting clear exit strategies for public capital. To address these issues, several frameworks—such as those developed by the OECD and multilateral institutions—provide guidance on structuring, monitoring, and evaluating blended transactions.

When effectively implemented, blended finance structures can unlock significant resources for green investment, demonstrate project viability, and create pathways for future market-based financing. They remain a central tool in efforts to scale private sector engagement in climate and environmental action.

Co-financing Models and De-risking

Co-financing models are collaborative financing arrangements in which multiple stakeholders—typically a mix of public, private, and development finance institutions—jointly fund a project or program. In the context of green finance, co-financing plays a critical role in mobilizing capital, sharing risk, and building investor confidence in environmentally sustainable activities. These models are particularly valuable for large-scale or complex projects that require diverse expertise, long-term capital, and a risk-sharing approach.

Co-financing structures are designed to leverage the complementary strengths of different funding sources. Public or concessional capital often enters at an early stage, assuming higher risk to unlock subsequent private investment. This early-stage support may take the form of grants, subordinated debt, guarantees, or technical assistance. Private sector partners typically provide commercial financing once the project has demonstrated viability and risk has been reduced.

A common approach within co-financing models is risk layering, where different types of capital are deployed across a tiered structure based on the level of risk each participant is willing to accept. Public and philanthropic actors may take a junior or first-loss position, while private investors enter at senior levels with reduced exposure to default or project failure. This model enhances project bankability and attracts institutional capital that may otherwise avoid higher-risk opportunities.

De-risking strategies embedded in co-financing models are critical for addressing market failures and perceived barriers to investment. These strategies include credit enhancements, political risk insurance, currency hedging, and long-term off-take agreements. By reducing uncertainty, such tools help achieve more favorable financing terms and expand access to capital in challenging markets.

Co-financing is commonly used in sectors like renewable energy, climate-resilient infrastructure, and sustainable agriculture, where projects often require large upfront investment and operate in evolving policy environments. In these contexts, DFIs and MDBs frequently serve as anchor investors and project facilitators, helping align the interests of all parties.

To ensure effective implementation, co-financing arrangements require clear governance structures, transparency in financial terms, and alignment on environmental and social standards. Proper coordination among partners is essential for managing timelines, performance monitoring, and exit strategies.

In sum, co-financing models—when combined with targeted de-risking instruments—can significantly expand the scale and impact of green finance. They serve as practical mechanisms for aligning public and private resources in pursuit of shared environmental and climate goals.

Strategic Alignment with National Plans

Strategic alignment between green finance activities and national development and climate plans is essential for ensuring policy coherence, maximizing impact, and directing financial flows toward priority areas. By integrating green finance instruments with nationally determined contributions (NDCs), climate strategies, and sustainable development goals, governments and financial actors can enhance the effectiveness of public and private investments.

National plans—such as climate action plans, low-emission development strategies (LEDS), adaptation frameworks, and sectoral roadmaps—provide a foundation for identifying investment needs and policy priorities. Aligning green finance with these plans ensures that resources are deployed where they are most needed and that projects contribute to the achievement of long-term environmental and socio-economic objectives.

For public finance institutions and development finance providers, alignment with national plans is often a precondition for funding. Climate funds such as the GCF and Adaptation Fund require proposals to demonstrate consistency with national strategies and stakeholder consultations. This alignment promotes country ownership, policy integration, and accountability in the use of climate finance.

From a blended finance perspective, aligning investment vehicles and co-financing structures with national plans helps attract concessional and grant-based resources while ensuring projects are embedded within broader policy frameworks. Strategic alignment also supports regulatory harmonization, helping to reduce uncertainty for investors and improve the enabling environment for green finance.

Governments can facilitate alignment by developing green investment pipelines, publishing project lists tied to national goals, and establishing dedicated institutions or platforms to coordinate planning and financing. These tools help reduce transaction costs, improve project preparation, and signal readiness to international investors.

Private sector actors also benefit from alignment with national plans, as it enables them to identify priority areas for investment, anticipate policy developments, and enhance their contribution to national sustainability objectives. Financial institutions increasingly assess project alignment with NDCs and sustainable development targets as part of their ESG due diligence and impact assessment processes.

Strategic alignment is also critical for monitoring and reporting, as it provides a basis for measuring the contribution of financial flows to national and international commitments. By linking financial performance with climate and development metrics, stakeholders can assess effectiveness and guide resource allocation over time.

Overall, aligning green finance tools with national plans supports a coordinated, efficient, and goal-oriented approach to sustainability, strengthening the connection between financial instruments and long-term development pathways.

Chapter 9: Fintech, Digital Innovation, and Retail Green Finance

Fintech and digital innovation are reshaping the landscape of green finance by introducing new platforms, tools, and services that enhance transparency, accessibility, and efficiency. From blockchain-based green bonds to mobile applications that track carbon footprints, digital technologies are broadening participation and creating new opportunities for individuals and institutions to engage in sustainable finance. This chapter explores how fintech is driving innovation in green financial products, enabling real-time data use, and expanding access to green investment opportunities for retail investors. It also considers the potential and challenges of scaling digital solutions to support the global sustainability agenda.

Fintech for Green Finance

Financial technology (fintech) is increasingly being leveraged to support the development and expansion of green finance by offering digital tools that enhance efficiency, transparency, and access to sustainable financial products. Fintech solutions are applied across a wide range of financial services—including lending, investing, payments, and reporting—to facilitate environmentally sustainable practices and promote climate-aligned financial decision-making.

In green finance, fintech platforms support the mobilization of capital by simplifying investment processes and expanding participation. For example, digital crowdfunding platforms and peer-to-peer lending models enable individuals and small businesses to raise funds for renewable energy installations, energy efficiency upgrades, or sustainable agriculture projects. These platforms reduce transaction costs and open new channels for financing community-level green initiatives.

Fintech is also used to develop real-time data and analytics tools that help financial institutions and investors evaluate climate-related risks and opportunities. AI, machine learning, and big data are being employed to assess ESG performance, conduct automated sustainability scoring, and improve climate risk modeling. These technologies enable faster and more accurate decision-making and support compliance with emerging ESG disclosure requirements.

Another area of application is in the tokenization of green assets, where blockchain technology is used to represent ownership of sustainable investments such as green bonds, carbon credits, or renewable energy certificates. Blockchain enhances transparency, traceability, and security, which can increase investor confidence and reduce fraud in the green finance market.

Digital payment solutions are being linked to environmental outcomes as well. Some fintech companies offer products such as green credit cards that allocate a portion of spending toward tree planting or carbon offsetting. Others provide platforms that allow users to track their personal carbon footprint based on spending behavior and offer suggestions for emissions reductions or sustainable alternatives.

Despite the growing potential of fintech in green finance, several challenges remain. These include concerns about data privacy, regulatory oversight, interoperability, and equitable access to digital infrastructure. Addressing these challenges requires collaboration between innovators, regulators, and financial institutions to ensure that digital solutions are secure, inclusive, and aligned with environmental goals.

Overall, fintech represents a promising enabler of green finance innovation. By expanding access to sustainable financial products, improving the availability of environmental data, and supporting efficient capital flows, fintech contributes to the development of a more inclusive and technology-driven sustainable finance ecosystem.

Crowdfunding and P2P Lending

Crowdfunding and peer-to-peer (P2P) lending platforms offer alternative financing channels for environmentally sustainable projects by connecting fundraisers directly with individuals or institutional investors. These digital models bypass traditional intermediaries such as banks, enabling a more decentralized and accessible form of green finance. Their application in the green finance space has grown as demand for community-based and impact-driven investment opportunities continues to rise.

Crowdfunding refers to the practice of raising small amounts of capital from a large number of contributors, typically via online platforms. In the context of green finance, crowdfunding can be used to fund projects such as rooftop solar installations, energy-efficient housing, organic farming, reforestation initiatives, or clean technology start-ups. Campaigns may offer contributors financial returns (investment-based crowdfunding), rewards (such as products or services), or social recognition for supporting environmental outcomes.

Investment-based crowdfunding platforms allow individuals to invest directly in green enterprises or projects in exchange for equity or debt instruments. These platforms typically conduct basic due diligence, provide project information, and enable user-friendly interfaces for transaction management. The lower entry threshold makes it possible for retail investors to participate in sustainability-focused investments, expanding access beyond institutional markets.

Peer-to-peer lending models operate similarly but focus specifically on debt financing. Through P2P platforms, borrowers—such as individuals, small businesses, or project developers—can obtain loans funded by multiple individual lenders. Interest rates are generally determined by platform algorithms based on borrower creditworthiness and risk profiles. In the green finance space, P2P lending has been used to support projects such as off-grid solar systems, energy efficiency retrofits, or sustainable mobility solutions.

These models provide several benefits for sustainable finance. They increase access to capital for small-scale or early-stage projects that may not meet conventional bank lending criteria, and they enable retail investors to align their investments with environmental values. Furthermore, the transparency and interactivity of crowdfunding platforms help raise awareness and build public engagement around sustainability issues.

However, there are also challenges. Regulatory oversight varies significantly by jurisdiction, and investor protection mechanisms may be limited compared to traditional finance. Platform reliability, project screening standards, and risk disclosure practices also differ, which can affect credibility and investor confidence.

As crowdfunding and P2P lending evolve, efforts are underway to improve governance, enhance due diligence processes, and encourage integration with broader sustainable finance strategies. When supported by appropriate safeguards and aligned with environmental goals, these digital financing models can play a valuable role in mobilizing grassroots support and capital for green initiatives.

Blockchain and Tokenization of Green Assets

Blockchain technology and the tokenization of green assets are emerging as innovative tools in the sustainable finance space, offering increased transparency, traceability, and accessibility in the management and trading of environmentally aligned financial instruments. These technologies have the potential to streamline processes, lower transaction costs, and broaden participation in green finance by enabling secure and verifiable digital representation of assets.

Blockchain is a type of distributed ledger technology (DLT) that records transactions in a secure, decentralized, and tamper-resistant manner. In green finance, blockchain applications are being explored across several areas, including issuance and tracking of green bonds, carbon credit registries, renewable energy certificates, and impact reporting systems. The immutability and auditability of blockchain records make it especially valuable for verifying environmental claims and preventing double counting in markets such as voluntary carbon offsets.

Tokenization refers to the process of converting rights to a real-world asset into a digital token on a blockchain. In the context of green finance, tokenized assets may include shares in renewable energy projects, verified carbon credits, or units of environmental impact (e.g., avoided emissions). These tokens can be traded on digital platforms, allowing for fractional ownership and improved liquidity. This can lower the investment threshold and enable greater retail and institutional participation in green asset markets.

Tokenization also supports automation and efficiency through the use of smart contracts—self-executing agreements that operate based on coded conditions. For example, a smart contract could automatically release funds upon verification of an environmental milestone, such as the generation of a certain amount of clean electricity or the issuance of a certified carbon credit.

While the benefits are promising, the application of blockchain and tokenization in green finance is still at an early stage. Key challenges include regulatory uncertainty, limited interoperability between platforms, and the need for high-quality, verifiable underlying data. Environmental integrity depends on the robustness of the data feeding into blockchain systems, which in turn requires strong third-party verification and governance standards.

Moreover, blockchain's environmental footprint has been a topic of debate, especially with respect to energy-intensive consensus mechanisms like proof-of-work. However, more energy-efficient alternatives, such as proof-of-stake, are increasingly being adopted in sustainability-oriented projects.

As standards evolve and technological adoption increases, blockchain and tokenization could become integral components of digital green finance infrastructure. By improving trust, reducing friction, and enabling innovative financing models, these tools can support the scaling and democratization of environmentally sustainable investment.

ESG Robo-Advisors and AI Tools

ESG robo-advisors and AI tools are playing an increasingly important role in the personalization, scalability, and integration of sustainability considerations in investment decision-making. These digital tools use algorithms and data-driven models to automate portfolio construction, align investments with ESG preferences, and streamline ESG analysis across asset classes.

Robo-advisors are digital platforms that offer automated, algorithm-based financial planning and investment management services with minimal human intervention. ESG-focused robo-advisors incorporate sustainability filters into their investment algorithms, allowing users—particularly retail investors—to select portfolios that reflect their ethical or environmental values. Users can typically adjust their risk tolerance, sustainability priorities, and financial goals to receive customized portfolio allocations that emphasize low-carbon, resource-efficient, or socially responsible investments.

These platforms enhance accessibility to ESG investing by lowering costs, simplifying user interfaces, and offering fractional shares in sustainable funds. They also contribute to the democratization of green finance, providing retail investors with tools traditionally used by professional wealth managers.

In parallel, AI tools are being used by institutional investors and asset managers to analyze vast amounts of ESG data, identify trends, and enhance risk assessment. Natural language processing (NLP) allows AI systems to extract ESG-related information from unstructured sources such as news articles, company reports, and regulatory filings. Machine learning algorithms can detect patterns in ESG performance, forecast sustainability risks, and optimize asset allocations in line with sustainability objectives.

These technologies are particularly useful for ESG scoring, where AI models evaluate companies based on multiple indicators across environmental, social, and governance dimensions. AI can help reduce reliance on inconsistent or incomplete self-reported data by identifying discrepancies or validating claims through third-party sources.

Despite their benefits, ESG robo-advisors and AI tools face several challenges. These include the lack of standardized ESG data, potential algorithmic bias, and limited transparency in how sustainability metrics are weighted or interpreted. Ensuring user trust and regulatory compliance is essential, particularly as these tools influence a growing share of investment flows.

As digital finance continues to evolve, ESG robo-advisors and AI tools are expected to become more sophisticated and widely adopted. When supported by reliable data and robust governance, they can enhance the integration of sustainability into everyday investment decisions and institutional portfolio management.

Retail Green Finance Products

Retail green finance products provide individuals with the opportunity to contribute to environmental sustainability through personal financial decisions. These products are designed for non-institutional investors and everyday consumers, enabling broader participation in the green finance ecosystem. As awareness of climate change and sustainability grows, demand for accessible, transparent, and impactful retail green finance offerings continues to increase.

One of the most widely recognized retail products is the green bond for individual investors, often issued by governments, development banks, or financial institutions. These instruments raise capital for environmentally beneficial projects such as renewable energy, sustainable transport, or reforestation. In some cases, retail green bonds are offered with lower minimum investment thresholds, simplified access through digital platforms, and clear environmental use-of-proceeds reporting to attract non-professional investors.

Retail green finance also includes green savings accounts and green term deposits, which function like traditional deposit products but ensure that the funds are allocated to green lending portfolios. Banks offering these products may publish impact reports detailing the types of projects financed, helping to increase transparency and consumer trust. These products appeal to environmentally conscious savers who wish to align their savings behavior with their values.

Another growing category includes green investment funds and ETFs marketed to retail clients. These funds invest in companies or assets that meet predefined sustainability criteria and are often accessible through robo-advisors, brokerage platforms, or employer-sponsored retirement plans. Green ETFs, in particular, offer diversified exposure to sectors such as clean energy, water management, and circular economy solutions.

Some financial institutions also offer green credit cards or loyalty programs, where a portion of transaction fees supports environmental initiatives such as tree planting or conservation efforts. Additionally, mobile apps are emerging that track personal carbon footprints based on spending patterns, helping users understand and potentially offset their environmental impact.

While retail green finance products increase market participation, several challenges remain. These include ensuring product credibility, preventing greenwashing, and providing clear, comparable information on environmental benefits. Regulatory frameworks and voluntary standards are evolving to improve disclosure and safeguard consumer interests.

Overall, retail green finance products serve as a valuable entry point for individuals to support sustainable development through their financial choices. By aligning everyday financial behavior with environmental goals, these products contribute to a more inclusive and participatory approach to green finance.

Digital Inclusion and Democratization of Green Finance

Digital inclusion is a key enabler of the democratization of green finance, allowing broader participation in environmentally sustainable financial products and services. As digital technologies reshape financial markets, ensuring equitable access to digital platforms and tools becomes essential for expanding the reach and impact of green finance. When inclusively designed, digital solutions can empower individuals, small businesses, and underserved communities to engage with sustainability-oriented investments and financial services.

Democratization in this context refers to the removal of traditional barriers to green finance participation, such as high minimum investment requirements, limited financial literacy, and geographic or institutional constraints. Digital platforms—including mobile banking, fintech applications, and online investment tools—are lowering these barriers by offering simplified user interfaces, fractional investments, and remote access to sustainable financial products.

Mobile-based platforms and app-based fintech services have made it possible for users in remote or low-income areas to access green loans, participate in crowdfunding campaigns, or invest in renewable energy projects. These platforms are particularly impactful in emerging markets, where conventional financial infrastructure may be limited. For example, pay-as-you-go solar energy systems enabled by mobile payments have improved energy access while promoting financial inclusion and environmental sustainability.

Financial literacy and digital skills remain essential to ensuring that digital green finance tools are used effectively and responsibly. Efforts to promote user education, build trust in digital systems, and provide customer support are critical components of inclusive digital finance strategies. Public-private partnerships, NGOs, and multilateral organizations are often involved in delivering digital literacy programs and promoting ethical fintech development.

However, risks such as unequal digital access, data privacy concerns, and algorithmic bias must be addressed. Without targeted efforts to overcome these challenges, digital transformation could reinforce existing inequalities rather than reduce them. Governments and regulators play a key role in setting standards, promoting interoperability, and ensuring that digital finance infrastructure is both accessible and secure.

Ultimately, digital inclusion supports the scaling of green finance by opening participation to a more diverse base of users. It enables retail investors, small enterprises, and underbanked populations to contribute to and benefit from the transition to a low-carbon, sustainable economy. When designed with inclusion in mind, digital innovations have the potential to make green finance more participatory, equitable, and effective.

Conclusion

This book has examined a broad range of tools used to support the growth and effectiveness of green finance. These include well-established instruments such as green bonds, sustainability-linked loans, and green investment funds, which mobilize capital for environmentally aligned activities through structured finance. Other mechanisms, like carbon markets and offsetting schemes, use market-based approaches to price emissions and support climate mitigation efforts.

Risk mitigation instruments, including guarantees, insurance, and blended finance, address barriers to investment by sharing or reducing financial exposure. In parallel, frameworks such as taxonomies, disclosure standards, and impact measurement systems provide clarity, transparency, and accountability in identifying and assessing green activities.

Innovative technologies—from blockchain-based asset tokenization to ESG robo-advisors—are expanding access to green finance and increasing data-driven decision-making. These tools are complemented by policy-driven mechanisms like green public procurement, budgeting, and strategic alignment with national plans, which help anchor green finance within broader development agendas.

Together, these tools form a growing ecosystem that supports the allocation of capital toward environmentally sustainable outcomes across both institutional and retail financial markets.

Integration and Systems Thinking

Effective green finance does not rely on isolated instruments but rather on the integration of multiple tools within a coherent system. Finance must operate alongside environmental policy, technological innovation, and institutional frameworks to drive meaningful outcomes. For example, a green bond issuance is most effective when aligned with credible taxonomies, subject to transparent disclosure, and supported by risk-sharing arrangements or public incentives.

Systems thinking also requires considering the interconnections between environmental, social, and economic dimensions, especially when designing and applying financial tools. Ensuring that environmental goals are pursued without unintended social or economic consequences is vital for long-term impact and policy coherence.

Building synergy across instruments—such as combining digital platforms with green guarantees or aligning public finance with private-sector blended models—can amplify the reach and effectiveness of green finance. Integrated approaches are essential to support the transition to sustainable economies at scale and across diverse contexts.

Call for Innovation and Global Coordination

Scaling green finance to meet global sustainability goals requires continued innovation, as well as stronger coordination across borders, sectors, and institutions. New financial products, business models, and data technologies must evolve in response to shifting climate and environmental priorities. At the same time, ensuring integrity, accessibility, and inclusivity remains essential.

Global coordination is increasingly important as financial markets become more interconnected and sustainability challenges transcend national boundaries. Alignment of taxonomies, disclosure standards, and reporting practices can reduce fragmentation, improve comparability, and facilitate cross-border investment. International organizations, development finance institutions, regulators, and the private sector all have a role in driving convergence and capacity building.

Ultimately, meeting the climate and sustainability challenge will depend not only on how much finance is mobilized, but also on how effectively tools are designed, combined, and applied. Continued commitment to innovation, collaboration, and learning will be key to advancing green finance in a complex and rapidly evolving global landscape.

www.ingramcontent.com/pod-product-compliance
Lightning Source LLC
Chambersburg PA
CBHW071607200326
41519CB00021BB/6907